Life After Lemonade

by

April Capil

*"Work out your own salvation,
with fear and trembling."*

- Phillippians 2:12

Introduction

In *Recipe For Lemonade*, I shared my strategies for crisis management: how to make it through a tough time without (for lack of a better phrase) *losing your shit*. In one year, I lost my small business, was diagnosed with Stage 3 cancer, and realized I was probably going to lose my dream home (and really, my dream *life*) on a tropical island that I had – ironically - just picked up everything to move to. In the aftermath of this string of falling dominoes, I floundered, and stumbled, and struggled, until one day, I realized I was... not *home*, exactly, but... *out of the woods*. Out of the woods, and in one piece. My journey was finally over.

Or was it?

I wasn't in chemo, but I was still haunted by the possibility of a recurrence. I'd short-sold my house and wasn't struggling to pay my mortgage anymore, but I had new worries: making a living and identifying where I was going to make that living in. The pithy tips and tricks I'd written about in my first book – being honest with myself about my expectations, finding perspective, and counting my blessings – had worked to keep me sane through a crisis, but despite being out of the woods, I still didn't feel like I was quite *home* yet. It was as if I was living in a limbo-like "half-life," caught between a world that was in ruins, and a "new normal" I was *supposed* to be living in, but didn't have a map to *get* to. I felt like a traveler who'd crossed a canyon, then watched in horror as the bridge behind her burned, blocking any path of return. *How do I get back home?* I found myself wondering. I certainly couldn't retrace my steps. Was it even *possible* to feel "normal" again, and was I crazy for thinking I could?

And then, a funny thing happened.

After I finished *Recipe For Lemonade*, I started reading a lot of Joseph Campbell. Considered one of the world's leading experts on mythology, Campbell wrote primarily about the "Hero's Journey" – a kind of mythic structure he proposed all stories follow, whether you are talking about the Bible or *Star Wars*. The Hero's Journey, Campbell argued, is a kind of storyline that leads a person down a path that is universal to human existence, because it is a path of growth and development. This path – this *journey* – of life, and death, and rebirth, is one that all human beings go through and experience, and because of this, we subconsciously recognize its patterns and milestones.

After reflecting on Campbell's work, I thought about my *own* "Hero's Journey" - how it began, where it took me, and most importantly, how far I'd come, in the aftermath of so much disaster. What I realized, looking back, was that I wasn't at the **end** of my journey. *I was only in the middle.* I had vanquished Sauron, but I was still in Mordor - miles and miles from the Shire, with no map telling me how to get back. No wonder I didn't feel like I'd reached my "new normal" – *I wasn't there yet.* I wasn't even close.

Beck Weathers, famous for his amazing survival after being left for dead on Mt. Everest, wasn't at the end of his journey when he got down to the Western Cwm of the mountain. Sure, he was in good hands, moments away from being airlifted out in a helicopter rescue that broke altitude records, but he was *months and miles* from being the man he was when he left home to climb the tallest peak in the world. Getting back to base camp was only *half* the journey.

There are a lot of resources out there on how to deal with a diagnosis of cancer, how to treat cancer you already have, and how to get through treatment in one piece. What I had trouble finding, while I was going through my own battle, was advice on what to do *after* treatment. I mean, my hair was coming back, but I didn't feel like my old self. How was I

4

supposed to wake up every day and still function like a normal person, knowing my cancer could come back too? How was I supposed to go back to being the person I was BEFORE cancer - someone I felt like I could never be again, having had it? Even when I started to *look* like me, I didn't *feel* like me. And as person after person came to me with stories about how my book had gotten them through losing a child, going through a divorce, or recovering from trauma, I realized that they were all in the same limbo I was: out of the woods, but not home yet.

Substitute "cancer" for any number of life-changing crises and you find that all survivors have the same two questions: The first is, *how do I get through this?* The second is, *how do I get back to where I was before this?*

This book is about the second question: *life*, after lemonade. How to get from *out of the woods* to *home safe*.

PART ONE:
THE HARD TRUTHS

Chapter One: The Future You Thought You Had

We are told, over and over, what we deserve, because of the decisions we've made. We are told that if we get the right education, if we make the right investment, if we marry the right person, that we are entitled to have whatever we want. It doesn't matter who's doing the telling, of course. Sometimes it's the TV, or your parents, or a poster on a Metro train. Sometimes, it's something you tell yourself, based on some story you've made up in your head or a dogma you believe in. After a while, we might start to believe that happiness is a combination to a safe – right 23, left 37, right 16. If we can just figure out the combination, if we can just do everything right, we tell ourselves, we'll never have to worry about anything, ever again. It seems perfectly logical – exactly like a Newtonian universe should be.

In May of 2008, I thought I'd figured out the combination to that bright and promising future. I had a Green MBA and a blossoming online business. I'd just quit my job to move to Kaua'i and start what I thought would be the next New Alchemy – a sustainable farm and education center where world-changers could come and hold charettes about green design and holistic living. I saw myself teaching at-risk youth about eco-friendly construction and reclaimed materials, and partnering with beyond-organic CSAs to develop a replicable model of food-to-table education programs. My business was going to change the way children thought about play, and cultivate a generation of resourceful, creative Americans who would grow up knowing how to think critically and systemically. I had already made so many of my dreams come true, I was confident that in a few short years, I would have the other pieces of the puzzle – a husband, children, and the financial security that a world-changing entrepreneur deserved.

A year later, I was jobless (my business had failed in the wake of the bailout), hairless (I was in my fifth month of chemotherapy), and my dream home in Kaua'i had fallen out of escrow for the first of four times (it eventually short-sold for half of what I paid for it). I had just gotten home from a horrible job interview, and was sitting at my kitchen table thinking, *This Isn't What Was Supposed To Happen.*

It's a rude awakening, when life doesn't serve up what you wanted. When you dance for rain and the clouds don't roll in. You might start to think you didn't dance hard enough, or long enough, or often enough. You might even start to think you DID something to deserve your misfortune, that it's God's punishment for your sins or your inadequacies. You might go the other way, and feel cheated and unjustly victimized by a vengeful deity. You might hate your Creator for unjustly screwing you over.

No matter what your reaction is, it's all the same thing: *you, telling yourself a story, to explain what happened.* That's it.

By the time I'd reached my two year cancer-free anniversary, I'd been through every emotion, analyzing my mistakes via rollercoasters of expectations and blame, and in the end, I came to realize a singular truth about life: *shit happens.* Shit happens, all the time, to good people who don't deserve it. Sometimes it's your fault, and sometimes it's not, and most of the time, there isn't a damn thing you can do about it but pick up the pieces and keep on going.

Of course I didn't do anything to *deserve* cancer, or bankruptcy, or unemployment, but when I looked back, and was **completely** honest with myself, I realized that while I had good intentions, I had made some ridiculous mistakes. I'd bought a house I couldn't afford. I'd made an $80,000 design error when I started my business – a mistake that, in a better economy, with the right partners or venture capital, I could have (as filmmaker Robert Rodriguez once put it) "waved the money hose at" and overcome, but in a serious recession, it was insurmountable. I'd also assumed, like my doctors had, that I was too young and healthy to get cancer, and I neglected to take my lump seriously. Who wants to have cancer? Not me – me, who was starting a business that was going to change the world, and moving to an island paradise to live a life others only dream about. *Looking back, my arrogance and naiveté* **astounds** *me*. My hindsight now isn't just 20/20; it's 3D, with stereo surround sound. Of *course* it all fell apart, I think. *Anyone* in my situation could have had the same result, given the same circumstances.

Now, if you've read *Recipe For Lemonade*, you know the first step towards making lemonade is doing what I just did: being honest with yourself about what your expectations were in a situation. There are more steps, of course, but the first one – *examining what you thought you deserved* – is often the most important, because it opens your eyes. It makes you see the kind of thinking that got you into this mess, and once you can look at your logic honestly, and most importantly, *without judgment*, you can put yourself on a path out of the woods.

After taking a good long look in the mirror, I knew exactly how I got into the woods in the first place. Since then, I've forgiven myself; I don't beat myself up for being human, for being short-sighted or naïve or arrogant. No, I didn't *deserve* misfortune, but could I see how it was *possible*, given the precarious position I'd put myself in, and the unrealistic expectations I'd had? Absolutely. My life falling apart wasn't a plot by the Universe to cheat me out of my dream future; it was just a *possibility*, given my circumstances and the choices I'd made. Owning that realization was the most important step in my recovery, and while it was disappointing and disheartening, once I stopped judging myself, it was also incredibly freeing.

Here's the other thing I realized: life is inherently uncontrollable and unpredictable. We look at horoscopes and plan ahead and make allowances, but at the end of the day, we're never *completely* in control. So all we can really do to protect our sanity is be prepared, learn to roll with the punches, and look for happiness whenever and wherever we can. Most importantly, we must do away with this pervasive belief that *the world owes us something.* **I don't care how bad a hand you've been dealt – the world doesn't owe you a thing.** I stumbled and fell down a mile into the Disney Princess Half Marathon and *not one person* stopped to see if I was okay. Should I have sat there and moaned about my hurty knee or scratched-up palm? Would it have gotten me to the finish line any faster? I picked myself up and kept running, and finished my first sub-3 hour half marathon. *The only way we move forward is by continuing to move forward.* It sounds like common sense, but when we fall down, we sometimes **wait** for someone to pick us up, rather than picking **ourselves** up, and that's how we end up getting stuck. What's worse, once you're stuck, you might even start to nurture a sense of *entitlement* – to rescue, to pity, to compensation – and that's what will *really* hold you back from moving forward.

If you've made it through a crisis, you've already made it out of the woods. But if you truly want to get *back home*, the first thing you must do is curb any stirrings of entitlement. Stop whining about how much you've been through or what you think you deserve *because* of what you've been through (*especially* if you think you deserve to be picked up and carried home by someone else!). Rather than waiting for someone to rescue you, you must pick yourself up, dust yourself off, and keep going. If you need help, ask for help. Accept help. But don't be a baby, and don't wallow. THIS is what real recovery looks like: moving forward, gaining traction, and building strength. Let your life be galvanized by a sense of purpose on your journey from the edge of the woods back to your front porch. Maintaining the belief that you deserve to be carried the rest of the way home, just because things have been ridiculously difficult up to this point, will *literally* not get you anywhere on this journey, **so drop your sense of entitlement right now.**

If you catch yourself telling a story about what you deserve because of what you've been through, I want you to stop and ask yourself one question: **Who told you that?** Who told you that if you went to school, you'd get a good job? That if you married the right person, you'd be happy? That if you sent your kids to the right school, your daughter wouldn't get pregnant? *Who told you that? And, more importantly, why did you believe them?*

You know why you believed them? *Because you wanted to.* Because we all want to. Because life is so much easier to navigate if all you have to do is pick a lock. Figure out the combination to a safe. Rub a lamp and get your wishes granted. Well, I'm here to tell you – *that ain't life, friends. That's not how it works.*

The most painful magical thinking that we can get sucked into is what I call time machine logic. When something happens, taking away our chance at the future we thought we had, we want so badly to believe that there is something we can do to get back what we've lost. We start to think there *must* be a way to go back to the life we had, before we ever set foot in the woods. But we can't go backwards in life – only forwards. We struggle against our reality, and might even start to think that if we can BE that person we were, we can HAVE the future that we were going to have. It's hard to let go of that dream that got Nagasaki-ed when you went into the woods, isn't it? You tell yourself, "If I can just **be** the person I was **before**, I can **have** the future I had **before**." But the world just doesn't work that way, my friends. *Your high school prom dress isn't a time machine. Fitting in it will not take you back to 1982.*

Whether you like it or not, surviving something changes you – sometimes a little; sometimes a lot. That life, and the person you were before all this, are **GONE**, and *they are never coming back*. It can be heartbreaking to accept, I know! The future you thought you had BECAUSE of who you were before all this – that's all gone too (but really, it was never a sure thing anyway, was it?). You can "go home," but *you* will be different, and *it* will be different, and no sense of entitlement over how bad or tough or unfair you've had it is going to change that. **The hardest part of finding your "new normal" will be letting go of the "old normal" and accepting that** *the future you thought you were going to have is going to be different, because YOU are different.*

Doctors call "recovery" a "return to the pre-disease state," which I think is misleading. Pre-disease, most people don't think they *can* get cancer. Most people, pre-disease, believe in a world where if you are good and kind and don't hurt anyone, not only *would* nothing bad happen to you; nothing bad *could* happen to you. So, when you are good and kind and you DO get cancer, or are hit by a drunk driver, or your child is abducted, it's not only hard to accept; it's even harder to return to the state of mind that you were in **before** your world fell apart, because that state of mind is innocent, and naïve, and even arrogant. It is a state of ignorant bliss compared to the reality being shoved down your throat now!

You've survived; you're alive, but now, you have to figure out how to go on living in a world that not only isn't the world you knew, it's a world that isn't GOING to EVER be the world that you *thought* it would be. It's an unfriendly, unexpected world - uncontrollable and unpredictable. "Recovery" is not as simple as jump-starting a heart with an AED. For most people, returning to the "pre-disease" state *would* require a time machine (and selective amnesia).

Sometimes, it helps to start by saying "comeback" instead of "recovery." Don't think of it as a journey to "recover" (to get back) something you've lost. Think of it like you're *coming home* after *being away.* To comeback, start by acknowledging what you've lost, and grieve for it so you can stop wasting time and energy trying to *recover* it. Maybe you lost a breast, or your sight, or a fiancée. Maybe it's your innocence that you lost - your belief in a world where good people don't get hurt. Whatever it is, *you have to let go of it to move forward*, or it will drag you down like an anchor, keeping you attached to the past. If you harbor a sense of entitlement that you somehow deserve to have it back, that is not going to help you – *it's going to trap you in a place of unhappiness*, because you will be unable to reconcile what **is** with what you think **should be**. Mourn what you've lost; have a wake for it, but *say goodbye*, and mean it. Let go.

If the stages of grief don't work for you, I suggest reading Freud's analysis of the process in his seminal work "Mourning and Melancholia" (1917), where he says (and I'm paraphrasing here) that the process of grief is not about wanting something that has been lost to *return*, but about transforming the feelings you have for the object (be they love, pride, or affection) into feelings that continue to exist, but *for something that is gone.*

It took me years to do this with my father, who died when I was 21. Month after month, I was torn apart by the sadness of his being gone, unable to look at pictures or revisit memories without simultaneously revisiting the pain of losing him. I lived a half-life, wanting every day to wake up from what felt like a horrible dream. After reading Freud's essay in one of my Film Studies classes, I gave myself permission to think of my father as a wonderful part of my life - but a part that had come to an end. I told myself, "I can be sad that he is no longer here, or I can be happy that I had him in my life at all." Of course I have moments of sadness even now, when I think about how his time here was cut short, but by learning to love him as someone who *is gone and is not coming back,* **I am no longer trapped in a world that I want to be different.** I accept that he is gone, and choose instead to be thankful I had him in my life as long as I did.

Grief *exists* because of our connection to these objects and people we've lost. It's natural to feel that when they depart, a part of our self has gone with them. Sometimes, the part that goes with them is so big, it tries to pull the rest of us in with it, and we struggle to survive. To fight against this is actually quite narcissistic: grief is a form of reckoning with our own survival instinct. The irony is, the only way we can literally survive the loss of an object is by letting go of it, by releasing this thing that we think we cannot bear the loss of. Otherwise, we follow it into death.

Sometimes, it's easier to let go of a **person** than it is to let go of a **dream**, which is why letting go of the future you thought you were going to have may be the hardest thing you've ever done, the hardest thing you will ever do. You *must*, though. If you want to make it back home, you have to let go of that imaginary future. Focus on today, and hang onto your survival instinct.

You can bear it, trust me. Losing something that was a part of you is not the same as losing yourself, unless you insist on going down with the ship. I have lost parents, best friends, time, money, houses and businesses, and none of these losses has cost me my life. **Human beings can bear losing just about anything, as long as they want to live.**

You can have another future worth living for. Imagine if Aron Ralston had clung to his dead limb, unable to imagine a future without it. He'd have lost his life, and not just his arm.

Chapter Two: No One Here Gets Out Alive

It's one of the most famous scenes in cinema: Superman, having given up his powers to be with Lois Lane, confronts a thug in a diner when he insults her. The thug throws him through a window, and as Lois helps the former Man of Steel collect himself, he wipes his mouth and stares incredulously at his hand. "Blood... my blood..." he says, stunned. With maybe a little chagrin, he realizes what he's become: the Man of Steel, now a man of flesh.

The second phase of survivorship is what I call "Accepting the Inevitability of Death." Really, it should just be called "Acknowledging Mortality," because the fact is, no one here gets out alive. It's news to most people, that they're mortal. We act like Superman, staring dumbfounded at our own blood. *I bleed?* Yep, that's right - *you bleed.* You don't have any insurance against tragedy, against disappointment or unmet expectations or plane crashes. Pile up all the statistics you want - you can still be that one in a million person in the wrong place at the wrong time, and there's nothing you can do about it, because guess what? *That's life.* It begins, it ends, and nothing in between is guaranteed.

Reckoning with life's unpredictability and uncontrollability is the second stage of survivorship because once you've acknowledged and accepted the loss of something you didn't think you *could* lose, you have to face the fact that you can lose *other* things, including the time you – and yes, your loved ones – have left on this planet. When my mother died, and my father died twelve years later, I was like Superman, incredulous. *I can lose **both** parents?* I felt cheated, betrayed, lied to. I felt unjustly traumatized, but the fact is, *kids lose both their parents every day.* Dozens of children in Rwanda lost them all in **one** day, horribly, brutally, and without warning. We all lose both our parents eventually, yet there I was, angry and hurt because it happened sooner than I'd expected.

You see, growing up, I held the belief that although children are orphaned all the time on the news and in stories, *surely I would never be one of those kids*. There's actually a name for this kind of thinking – it's called the Lake Woebegone Effect – when a person believes that bad things *do* happen, but they happen to *other* people. This naïveté, of course, is not exclusive to children. Our own country, in the wake of 9/11 was shell-shocked – positively *horrified* that a terrorist attack could happen *here*, even though it had happened years before, in the exact same building! Why were people surprised? Because 9/11 reminded us that bad things happen, and they can happen here, and now, without warning, to people who don't deserve it.

Surviving something life-threatening means acknowledging the heaviest of realizations: **that you could have died**. That's pretty heavy stuff, kids. Whether your life "flashes before your eyes" or not, you might think differently once it sinks in that this little parentheses we have here is just that - a window, an hourglass - and that there are no do-overs. Before cancer, I was Superman, but the moment my oncologist told me that not only did I have cancer, but that I had to do everything I could to keep it from coming back, I became Clark Kent, sitting in that diner, staring blankly at the blood on my hand. You mean I'm *mortal?* **I can bleed?** And in the months and years since, every time I have an unexpected injury, every time I have a headache that doesn't go away, or a weakness I'm not familiar with, I'm faced with the same reality: *I can die*. I don't live with a fear of dying, but I live with an awareness that I **can** die, despite all my efforts to stay alive, and while this is frightening sometimes, it makes me extremely grateful for the time I *get* to be here, because I never forget it's limited.

The strangest part is, when you've survived something, you go back to your life as you knew it and suddenly, you feel like Clark Kent in a **world** of Supermen: people start treating you like you're somehow more vulnerable than they are to the dangers of living. All of a sudden, you have to eat an apple every day and button up your overcoat, like you're the only mortal in the room (you might, at this point, want to scream, *"You know, YOU CAN BLEED TOO!"*). Another thing that happens is, *you* might start being overly cautious with yourself – avoiding things you were never afraid of before, because you no longer harbor this delusion that you're Superman. It could be minor things - like hydrogenated oils or high fructose corn syrup. It might be major things - like, moving too far away from your oncologist or getting on a cross-country airplane. Men of Steel don't have to fear injury, but Clark Kent? Clark can bleed. And since you've already bled once, why tempt fate?

What's important to remember, as you reckon with this stage of survivorship is, you're not made of steel, but you're not made of glass either. Life is a terminal disease, yes, but remind yourself: **you're not dead yet** (cue *Monty Python* joke). It's easy to walk around like the other shoe is going to drop, preparing for a future where cancer might come back, where another baby might be miscarried, where someone else can break your heart, but *why waste what little life you have left on this earth preparing for disaster to strike again?* Disaster may strike; it may not. Chances are, you probably won't see it coming, even if it does. I spent a lot of time post-treatment asking myself, "What happens if my cancer comes back?" until a nurse asked me, *"What if it doesn't?"* I realized that I really was living like I was dying - **but that I should be living like I was living.** There's a difference between knowing your life is going to end someday, and living like that end is imminent. So strive for a balance: acknowledge your mortality, but remember: *you're still alive.*

Chapter Three: To Be, Or Not To Be (That Is The Question)

To be, or not to be, that is the question:
Whether 'tis nobler in the mind to suffer
The slings and arrows of outrageous fortune,
Or to take arms against a sea of troubles
And by opposing end them. To die — to sleep,
No more; and by a sleep to say we end
The heart-ache and the thousand natural shocks
That flesh is heir to: 'tis a consummation
Devoutly to be wish'd. To die, to sleep;
To sleep, perchance to dream — ay, there's the rub:
For in that sleep of death what dreams may come,
When we have shuffled off this mortal coil,
Must give us pause — there's the respect
That makes calamity of so long life.
For who would bear the whips and scorns of time,
Th'oppressor's wrong, the proud man's contumely,
The pangs of dispriz'd love, the law's delay,
The insolence of office, and the spurns
That patient merit of th'unworthy takes,
When he himself might his quietus make
With a bare bodkin? Who would fardels bear,
To grunt and sweat under a weary life,
But that the dread of something after death,
The undiscovere'd country, from whose bourn
No traveller returns, puzzles the will,
And makes us rather bear those ills we have
Than fly to others that we know not of?
Thus conscience does make cowards of us all,
And thus the native hue of resolution
Is sicklied o'er with the pale cast of thought,
And enterprises of great pitch and moment
With this regard their currents turn awry
And lose the name of action.

- *Hamlet*, William Shakespeare

I post the whole of Hamlet's soliloquy here because there isn't a part I think I could take out without reducing the impact of it. He covers it all: to live, to die; suffering and why we suffer; how easy it is to end it all, and why we don't. In a single monologue, Shakespeare covers the dilemma of human existence: *why do we bother going on, when life can be so hard?*

The Third Phase of Survivorship is a serious one; I'm not going to sugarcoat it. Sometimes, you stumble into it in the midst of your trauma. Most people get to it after, when the imminent part of the crisis is over and their body is knitting itself back together. Usually, when you get to this phase, life is, for all intents and purposes, getting back to the way it was.

The thing is, it's *not* as it was, is it? It kind of *sucks*, actually. You're not Lance Armstrong, made stronger by cancer, winning Tour de Frances left and right. You're months, maybe years away from that point, because right now, you're just a twenty-something cyclist, fresh out of chemo, dropped from your team with everyone whispering that you'll never race again. You may not even be able to *imagine* a day when you'll race again, though you wouldn't admit it, for fear of letting everyone down. When you get to this phase, your life is probably WORSE than it was before - harder, harsher, and more disappointing, because of what you've been through. Even as your family and friends are cheering your recovery in the hopes that you'll be "back to your old self again," inside, you're wondering if life will ever be *worth living* again. It's heartbreaking, realizing how far you've fallen from where you were, and it's even more heartbreaking to face people who have never been where you are right now. You're asking yourself a million questions, and the one that comes up most often is, *why should I bother going on*?

To be, or not to be. That's the question we ask ourselves in this stage. Not "What will I do?" or "How will I get my life back?" or "Why is this happening?" All of that is secondary to the only thing that matters, which is **do you want to be?** Not to be *here*, not to *be where you used to be*, but just to even *be* at all. You might not even want to ask the question, because you're afraid the answer might be NO. *NO*, I don't want to be, because my lover is dead, because my breast is gone, because this FEMA trailer isn't as nice as my house was. NO, you might want to say, LIFE IS NOT WORTH LIVING ANYMORE because it's never going to be as good as it was before it all fell apart. That's a scary thought to have, because it means you survived disaster... for nothing. It makes you think, what was I fighting for, if not the chance to go on living?

It's okay to think this. Believe me, *I've thought this*. I've fought tooth and nail for my life, only to get to a point where I could barely come up with a reason not to end it. Most people who survive a tragedy inevitably find themselves thinking this, because frankly, it's no picnic rebuilding your life after it's fallen apart. When you meet ridiculous heart-wrenching resistance *on top* of unrelenting disappointment, it's only natural to want to give up. Hamlet's life was turned upside down, and it made him ask himself, *"Why go on? Why be here?"* If you want to go on living, you have to ask yourself the same question, because it's the only way you're going to know if you have it in you to *keep* going.

What's important to remember is, there is a difference between wanting to sit on the bench for a while, and wanting the game to be over. After disaster, when you're facing a future that is not what you thought it would be, *you must ask yourself if it's worth sticking around for.* "To be, or not to be?" is the only question that forces you to look inside yourself and measure the value of your future, however unpredictable it may be. It requires you to differentiate between being *tired* and being *done*, and trust me, there is *massive* difference.

Life is not always going to be easy. It's not always going to serve up what you want, no matter how hard you've had it or how hard you've worked for it. When you are in the process of putting Humpty-Dumpty back together again, you're going to face roadblocks and setbacks – the "slings and arrows" Shakespeare talks about – and no matter how positive a person you are, you're going to reach a point where you want to give up. Asking yourself, "To be, or not to be?" will force you to clarify what you mean by "giving up," and answering the question – honestly, and truly – will tell you what kind of a person you are. Are you the kind of person who is in it for the long haul, no matter how hard it gets, or are you the kind of person who really does have a limit of how much tragedy, pain, and disappointment they can take? Some people reach a point where they just cannot take it anymore, and when they do, they give up and check out. They ask, "To be, or not to be?" and decide to take their chances with "*the undiscovere'd country*," rather that stick around and wait to see if it gets better.

There is one truth that has saved my life every time I start to think it's not going to get any better: *we **don't know** what the future holds*.

When we're in a place of sadness and pain that seems like it's never going to end, what we forget is that it WILL end. *It will end*. NOTHING lasts forever – not pain, not happiness, and especially not suffering. Yes, we have a choice – to check out and end it sooner – but in ending the suffering, we also end our chance at any future happiness that may be in store for us.

Now, all this being said, you DO still have a choice. You always have a choice, even if you have a terminal disease, because YOU get to choose HOW you live, and that includes how long you live.

I have one caveat: if you hate your life because you feel cheated out of some better life, don't make everyone around you miserable with your negativity and self-loathing. Don't endanger other people with life-threatening behavior. If you can't bear it anymore, I say, either check the FUCK OUT or MAN UP and do something to make your situation better, if not more tolerable. You are not still alive just so you can scare everyone with a suicidal lifestyle, or whine about how tough it is for you to get through each day. *Trust me, there are people in this world who are having tougher days than you, my friend.*

If you're ALIVE, that means you GET TO LIVE. You have the privilege of still breathing on this planet. **Not everyone gets that choice.** Do you know how many mothers walk out their front door not knowing they're never going to get to see their children again? How many brothers lose their sisters and daughters and fathers and best friends to car accidents, train derailments, war, disease, and murder? Every SINGLE day, someone doesn't come home, and yet here you are, whining about how hard it is for you to go on living.

Survivorship is not just about whether you want to live or die; it's about how you are choosing to live the life you have left. So if you WANT to survive, you have to look in the mirror and ask yourself, are you going to live like someone who *wants* to be here, who *GETS* to be here, or someone who doesn't? Decide. Decide NOW, and commit to your decision.

Keep in mind, though, if you *don't* want to be here, you won't be for long. Maybe you'll take up chain smoking, or binge drinking, or hard drugs, and kill yourself slowly. Maybe you'll engage in risky behavior, and drive your car into a ravine or get bludgeoned in a bar fight. Maybe you'll stop exercising and start eating junk and your cancer will come back in ten places and chemo won't work anymore. And you know what? *When that happens, there is no do-over.* If you ask yourself the question, and decide you don't want to be here anymore, then change your mind later, it might be too late. So think carefully before you answer. Do you *really* not want to be here? Because if you decide that the life you're living is not *worth* living, you will start taking it for granted, and jeopardizing it in ways you can't even imagine.

I'm not saying that everyone who has a recurrence, or is in the wrong place at the wrong time WANTS to die. That's NOT what this is about at all. What this is about is allowing yourself to realize that whether you like it or not, you are going to be having this conversation with yourself every time your life isn't what it *used* to be – what you think it was SUPPOSED to be. Every time your day-to-day doesn't meet your expectations, you're going to start telling yourself a story that your life is worth less (worthless) compared to the life you were *going* to have. This little story may not seem destructive when it crops up at the checkout line, or when your car breaks down, or your supervisor belittles you, but when all three of these things happen on the same day, to someone who's been telling herself she doesn't WANT to be here, it's a recipe for suicide. And suicide doesn't have to be a gun to your head; it can be cutting someone out of your life that has been keeping your chin up, or getting high as a kite and plowing your car into a tree. *Suicide can be getting (or allowing yourself to get) to a place, through a series of disappointments and unmet expectations, where you just don't care if you live or die.* **And if you're not careful, if you're not paying attention, your apathy can make the choice for you.**

Remember this too: no man is an island. You can't deny the value of your life without denying the value of life itself, and while it's your choice to cherish it or throw it away, if you become careless with it, you will inevitably endanger the lives of people around you. You might be a firefighter with a death wish, who puts his coworkers at risk by rushing into unsafe situations. You might be a drug addict with a lover who would rather die with you than get clean and have a future. When you think about throwing your life away, think about the people you could take down with you, and consider the price: anyone who lives on the edge and doesn't value their life runs the risk of bringing someone with them when they go over, whether they intend to or not.

Some people would say, "Yes, I understand all this, but what about when you *want* to be here, but you just can't take the pain anymore?" You want to live, but you don't know if you can bear it, if it keeps going on like this. That's the hard part, right? Nope. That's the EASY part. *You want to live.* Let that sink in. If you *want* to *be*, then anything is manageable. Even if it gets hard or disappointing; if life gives you lemons, you can make lemonade. *As long as you want to live, you can fight for your life, and build a future worth living for.* You have no idea how strong you are, how long you can hang in there for, trust me. You can use the tools I'm going to share with you to suck it up and white knuckle it and keep moving until you're in a better place, but before ANY of that, *you have to want to be here*. I can give you all the strategies that have saved my life, but I can't make you want to fight for it – that's on you. So if you want to be here, *congratulations. THAT, we can work with. THAT'S* what this book is about – how to stick around. How to rebuild, and not give up when it gets hard. Because you know what? *It's going to be hard.*

It's going to be hard because even if you've decided you want to go on living, you will still meet women who seem wonderful and charming and doting, until they find out you can't have children because you're a testicular cancer survivor. You will still go on job interviews that give you hope about your future, until they tell you they can't hire someone with a criminal record. You will still spend hours dreaming about fantastic apartments that will never be yours because the landlord won't overlook your bankruptcy. When all of these lemons come pouring back into your life, you are going to want to tell yourself that you should have it easy because of everything that's happened to you, *but that is just not the way life works.* Rebuilding your life is not going to be any easier than building your life was in the first place; in fact, it's probably going to be harder. Prepare yourself for disappointment – don't *expect* it, but be *prepared* for it so you're not crushed when it comes. Decide that you won't let it derail or discourage you. Remind yourself that the world doesn't owe you a free ride just because you've had it hard, and build up the stamina you're going to need to move onwards and upwards. It is not going to be easy rebuilding your life, but you **can** do it, and you will be stronger and more tenacious because of it.

The good news is, eventually, an employer *will* take a chance on you, and you know what? You will value that chance for the miracle that it is. Eventually, a woman *will* appreciate you and adore you, and even have more faith in your than you ever had in yourself. Cultivate your tenacity and strength in the face of adversity. Persist, be optimistic, and keep trying. Don't give up when it gets hard, because trust me, *hard is inevitable*. If you persist, though, *triumph is inevitable too.* You will look out the window of a home you have dreamed of, and worked hard for, and feel pride and happiness again. Have faith in that, and it will carry you through the hard parts.

Remember, if you're still here, *you're still here.* It's important to remind yourself of that. What you need to do in this third stage of survivorship is craft a story you can tell yourself when you start to second-guess your decision to stick around. Tell yourself any story you want about *why* you're still here: that maybe someone Up There thinks you still deserve to be here, or that you still have "work to do" here, or that there are still things in your life left to experience. It doesn't matter, as long as it works for you. You're going to need something to hang onto when you start thinking about checking out, so if you truly want to live, craft a story that casts you as someone who *should* be here, who *wants* to be here, who is *meant* to be here. If you struggle, remind yourself that only someone who truly didn't value his or her life would end it, and if you are a survivor, there must be a part of you that wants to live. If you find yourself paralyzed with fear or dread, tap into that part of you that fought to survive. Life can be scary, but that doesn't mean it's not worth living. It's not scary all the time, right? Just some of the time? So, if you want to live; if, when you ask yourself, **to be or not to be**, the answer is, *to be*, and the only thing holding you back is a fear that life will always be this hard, remind yourself that nothing lasts forever… except death. Remember, life's difficulties are manageable and the intensity you feel right now will not last. Change is the one thing you *can* count on in life.

Now, once you make the decision that you WANT to be here, you need to stop screwing around and **LIVE** LIKE YOU WANT TO BE HERE. Consider yourself FORTUNATE that you had the strength, courage, luck, whatever, to make it through what you made it through in one piece and come out on the other side. Seriously. When you start feeling sulky and unappreciative of the gift that being here is, think about how many people DON'T GET to make it - the people who picked the wrong seat when they booked their ticket and didn't get to the emergency exit in time. Think about the literally hundreds of people who, each year, fall through the cracks of an imperfect medical system and are diagnosed too late to save their own lives. **You're here and they're not.** *You survived.* So count your (and pardon my French, but this is serious business) fucking blessings.

Once you have thought about it, and made the decision that you want to live, you have to get busy living. You have to stop acting like death is coming for you or life isn't worth living. You've asked the question, and answered it. If you still want to stick around, that means there is a part of you that believes that life IS worth living, so make a commitment to start acting like it, from this point forward.

PART TWO:
LIVES HALF-LIVED

Now that we've we talked about the Hard Truths, and you've faced the fact that the future you thought you were going to have is gone, hopefully you've done three things. First, you've begun to drop your sense of entitlement around *what you deserve* because of what you've been through. Second, you've accepted the reality that no one here gets out alive – that this window you have here on earth is all you've got, and there are no do-overs. Third – given that your future will most likely be different, and this is all the life you have left – you've asked yourself if the life you *do* have left is worth sticking around for.

If you've faced these truths, and decided that yes, the rest of your life IS worth sticking around for, then you're ready for the next step: getting busy living.

Getting busy living, unfortunately, is not always as easy as it sounds. There are three things that can hold us back – the temptation to stall while we "work on ourselves," the desire to "take it easy" after such a rough go, and worst of all, the delusion that we must give up our dreams in exchange for the security that accompanies a life without risk.

In this section of the book, I'm going to address these "limbos" we sometimes get stuck in, even after deciding to move on – ways we "half-live" by never committing to living our lives fully (all the while convincing ourselves that we have "made progress" after tragedy). When we half-live, we're not progressing, but existing in a kind of purgatory, stuck midway between giving up and moving on.

Some people talk themselves into staying in one of these "half-life" states forever, avoiding risk, and failure, and chance, because it saves them from being disappointed again. To live your life fully and deliberately means being yourself, challenging yourself, and embracing your dreams. This means risking being hurt, and even the strongest survivors can find that they just don't have it in them to survive something *else*. They trade in a **rich** life for a *safe* life, and make their peace with mediocrity.

At the end of this section, you will have to make another choice. You'll have to decide if you want to be content to check out, or you want to push yourself just a little further... and live a life worth surviving *for*.

Chapter Four: Development Hell

Before we begin this chapter, I'd like to paraphrase Baz Lurhman, who once wrote, *"When everything goes away, what you have left is your story."* Key to your recovery from disaster will be the **story** you're telling yourself, about who you are and why you're here.

I said in the previous chapter that the next step in rebuilding your life is crafting a story about your future. I know it's scary telling yourself a new story, for so many reasons. You don't want to imagine something that can be lost again. You might be unsure of who you are, because some trauma has messed with your head and made you second-guess yourself. For whatever reason, it can be a challenge to think about the next chapter of your life, and what it's going to be about.

Here is the truth: if you want to get back home, you have to start walking in a direction, and which way you go will depend on the **story** that you want your life to be about. The beautiful – truly, the most *amazing* – thing is, *you already know it*. It's been written on your heart since you were born, and no tragedy or disappointment can take it away or destroy it. This isn't some fruity-tooty fairytale B.S., either. *Everyone* on this earth is here for a purpose. Even the smallest blade of grass has a purpose, if only to turn sunlight into food so a cow can be nourished by it.

The hard part, of course, is living and believing in that purpose, because a lot of things get in the way of your discovery and acceptance of it. That's what this chapter is about.

My last weeks of chemo were not fun. I was hairless, jobless, and I had received a letter from my health insurance company announcing that they believed I had a pre-existing condition. Consequently, all claims related to my cancer treatment were being rejected. When you get a letter like that, any positive thinking you've been hanging onto… positively evaporates. What's worse, the stress of imagining how to pay off a quarter of a million dollars in medical bills gave me shingles on my tailbone, at a time when I was driving an hour four times a week to and from doctors' offices. I was at my wit's end physically and mentally, and my sister, seeing the distress I was in, took me with her to a three-day "Personal Power" camp in the hopes that it would give me back some of my optimism.

The camp *was* enlightening; I'll give it that. I met some wonderful people, and went through an exercise that made me truly grateful for having my sister in my life. What haunted me, though, was witnessing what a dangerous path "self-improvement" can put a person on, and a guy who was a perfect example of it.

We were sitting in a circle, talking about "next steps" in our lives – what we were going to take away from the seminar, that would help us grow and develop as human beings – and all of the speakers we'd heard from during the week were pitching their *own* seminars ("Available For A Limited Time Now!") on various self-improvement techniques – hypnosis training, sales and marketing mastery, and so on.

As the evening wrapped up, one woman, whose husband weighed close to 400 pounds, got up to speak. By this time, most of us at camp knew that her husband, who had brought her to seminar after pricey seminar, seemed to be on a never-ending quest for "self-improvement" (almost as if he had replaced cheeseburgers with thousand-dollar power camps, I thought). Although he had showed some progress (he *had* lost 50 pounds in six months), she implied that they were quickly running out of available credit, with no end to this mission of personal development in sight. She seemed exasperated – and slightly terrified – that after months of classes in how to achieve your dream life, neither she nor her husband had actually achieved theirs. They had learned a lot and read a lot and practiced a lot, but here they were, living... kind of a nightmare, financially. *"This is all really great,"* she said, clearly trying not to sound ungrateful, *"but... well, when do you **stop**?"*

"Well," the speaker said smoothly, *"I'll ask you: when do **you** want to stop getting better? When do **you** want to stop wanting to be a better person, having more abundance in your life, achieving more of your dreams? Personally, I don't ever want to stop."*

I could almost hear the woman's heart fall into her stomach with the sickening splash of a Chapter 7 filing.

"Development Hell" is a place in Hollywood where stories get lost. When a script sells, it inevitably goes through rewrite after rewrite, like a foster child shuffled from one home to another. In the process, a script can lose the heart of its story – that defining voice that made it so wonderful in the first place. *Development* is supposed to tighten and streamline a story, distilling it to an essence that speaks to a universal human condition. It's a *focusing* tool.

Development *Hell,* on the other hand, is what happens when an effort to improve something becomes muddled by a complete *lack* of focus. The story, without a guiding force – a trajectory, if you will – deteriorates into a mish-mash of half-baked potential. Development Hell is a dozen different people trying to tell *their* story through someone else's. I call it Hell because when it's **your** story that's getting buried and diluted by well-intentioned people, not only do you not *recognize* you're stuck in a directionless loop; you actually believe you're making *progress.*

When a person goes through a crisis, it inevitably invites self-examination: "How did I get here? What did I do to deserve this?" and the classic, "Who am I?" This is why the story you're telling yourself is so important. It's easy to lose your story in the wake of disaster, so you need to know it before you leave the border of the woods and try to find your way back home. If you don't know who you are and where you're going, you might start to convince yourself that the solution to escaping trauma is *being someone else* – someone this nightmare didn't happen to, couldn't happen to. A major crisis can strike at the core of your spirit. If you don't know your story, you can end up trying to be someone else under the guise of "self-improvement." You can end up in Development Hell.

It's natural to want to be someone else when your life falls apart. Who wants to be Humpty Dumpty, picking pieces of himself up at the base of a wall? *"God,"* you think, *"I want to be anyone **but** me right now."*

When I saw at this guy at the seminar, I saw someone who couldn't *bear* to be himself. There he was, breaking his bank account like he was panning for gold, hoping that eventually, at one of these seminars, he would magically be transformed into someone other than the broke, fat guy he saw himself as. It was tragic, but even worse, it was *familiar*, because every survivor has been there, including me.

Development Hell isn't about wanting to be better. It seems like it is – who doesn't want to be healthier or more financially secure? But really, it's about wanting someone else to take responsibility for your life, because you're scared of what you've done with it. Development Hell is looking in the mirror and saying, "This is a terrible story. I'm going to bury it and pretend it never existed, and write a sequel to someone else's story, and cast myself as the lead."

One of the bravest women I know said to me once, "I want to be the next Oprah," and I said to her, "Why would you want to be a second-rate Oprah when you can be a first-rate **you**? Trust me; no one will ever be as great an Oprah as Oprah, but no one will ever be as great a YOU as *you* – it's who you were born to be, and who will ever be able to compete with that?"

We spend our lives running from ourselves, and when we make mistakes or get disappointed, we use these experiences as evidence to justify trying to be someone else. When you're scared of where you've been, and where you are, you're scared of where you're going, and you're not going to trust your own judgment. You'll see people who are successful – usually some picture of success that society or your parents or your friends have defined – and you'll think, "I should listen to *that* guy, because he obviously knows what he's doing." You'll tell yourself that if you do what he does, you'll get where he is, which is a helluva lot better that where you are.

In theory, this works. Sometimes it even works in practice. The problem is, when you follow someone *else's* dreams, you're following someone *else's* bliss. You're not listening to your inner voice, because you're scared of where you think it got you, and that makes you scared of where it might tell you to go next. Some guru comes along and says, "Follow me," and it kills two birds with one stone - absolving you of the responsibility of running your own life, and justifying that surrender with evidence of another person's success. You don't have a plan and they do. All you have to do is give up who you are, and try to be who *they* are. It seems so rational, doesn't it?

The hardest thing to be in the world is yourself. The world tells you that you should be anything *but* yourself, because who you are isn't *good enough*. I've spent a lot of time in my life trying to be *good enough*, and when I looked in the mirror at 34 and saw an entrepreneur with money in the bank, a house on an acre of paradise, and the strength to hike the first two miles of the Kalalau Trail, I thought I had reached my pinnacle. What I know now is that *all of that* wasn't *who I was*. Who I am is what was **left** when all that went away – when I lost my money, and my dream house, and my health, and my strength. Baz had it right: when you lose all your **stuff**, what you have left is your **story**. *Your story is who you are*, and letting it be replaced by someone *else's* story will only derail you on your journey back home. Listen to yourself. You know better than anyone else what you need, and what's good for you.

People talk about the Law of Attraction, and while I don't believe in some magical force that brings you everything you want if you put pictures on your wall, what I do believe is that **when you start listening to yourself, you turn your life in the direction of your bliss**. As Joseph Campbell said, "*[I]f you do follow your bliss, you put yourself on a kind of track that has been there all the while, waiting for you, and the life that you ought to be living is the one you are living. When you can see that, you begin to meet people who are in your field of bliss, and they open doors to you. I say, follow your bliss and don't be afraid, and doors will open where you didn't know they were going to be.*"

Once I was out of treatment, I knew it was time to begin the process of rebuilding my life. The only problem was, I didn't know what kind of life to build. I couldn't go back to my old life, and I couldn't begin to imagine what a new one would even look like. How was I going to get a job or a place to live? I had always been driven and goal-oriented, but in the wake of losing so much, I felt lost and directionless. My little sister, who had been my only immediate family since she was 17 and I was 21, was baffled. Here was her big sister, who had always known what to do... floundering. She tried to help, of course, and sometimes this looked like telling me what I should and shouldn't eat. Sometimes, it looked like paying my cell phone bill for a year. We tried to be what we used to be, but as the months went on, our relationship grew more and more strained as she watched me – a peak-climber, if ever there was one – circle the foothills of Development Hell. I didn't know my story, I didn't know who I was or what I should be. I talked a lot about what I wanted to do, where I wanted to be, but I never seemed to gain any traction. Six months after my last chemo session, I was still working at a sporting goods store, and showing no signs of moving up or moving out. In desperation, I finally signed up for a First Descents climbing camp, hoping it would shake me out of the doldrums.

At camp, rock-climbing with a dozen other survivors, I saw that I wasn't alone in my struggles. I met other people who had lost everything, and heard their stories of how they'd knit their lives back together. I found a family that I was instantly a part of, and could not feel self-conscious around, because even though all our stories were different, they shared commonalities that made each one not seem so crazy, tragic, or unreal. For the first time in two years, I felt like my story wasn't one I needed to bury or be ashamed of. It was just another chapter on my journey, and one that was behind me.

When I came home, I was okay with myself, and even proud of myself, for being a survivor. I gave myself permission to listen to my inner voice, follow my bliss, and pen in hand, I began to write the next chapter of my life. I realized that I didn't want to be rich and famous and living in paradise and changing the world. What I wanted most of all was to be free, carrying very little on my back, meeting people I'd always wanted to meet. It was a crazy idea, and I knew it would be expensive and dangerous and potentially disastrous, but I took my car on a road trip.

In four months, I saw the United States from one end to the other, and surfed couches all along the way – couches of people I knew and people I didn't know. I didn't have a job or a plan, but I kept listening to myself, and when that voice told me it was time to stop and put down roots, I listened to it then too. I decided I wanted to live somewhere with clean air and clean water, where I could hike every weekend and walk to work, and even though it scared the crap out of me to follow a dream again, I did. And every day I come home to my little apartment in Boulder, six blocks from my office and a half-mile from a mountain, I thank that voice for encouraging me to follow my bliss, because it led me to a place that finally feels like home.

When you are standing at the edge of the woods and you've decided to start walking home, you may already know your story. It may feel like you are finally walking on a path you've known you should be walking on all along. If you can't feel it, if you can't hear your inner voice, you need to start listening. Go for a walk every day; listen to music that makes you feel good (and by "good," I mean, "not self-pitying or angry"). Write your feelings and fears and thoughts down in a journal, or trade in five minutes of television every day to meditate. If you quiet your mind enough to listen, you'll hear a voice telling you what you need to do and where you need to go, and that will be a start in the right direction.

Really "working on yourself" is just that: work. It's not as easy as subscribing to someone else's plan. YOU have to work up a sweat, YOU have to get your hands dirty, and YOU have to earn every victory along the way. But the beautiful thing is, they will be YOUR victories, YOUR triumphs. Listen to yourself and be yourself, because you're designed to be the best at it. It's scary to blaze your own trail, but it's like anything else: practice, and you'll get good at it.

In closing, take note: the biggest obstacles you will face on this road to being yourself will be the people you live and work with - your lovers and friends. Witnessing disaster can terrify people, and make them think about their own vulnerabilities. Even if a person loves you, if they see you crash and burn, they might think it's okay to approach you with suggestions on what you should do or who you should be to avoid these kinds of disaster in the future (when people would do this after I had cancer, I wanted to be like, IF YOU'RE SO FUCKING PSYCHIC, WHY DIDN'T YOU TELL ME TO TAKE THIS LUMP OUT FOUR YEARS AGO?). Now, some of these people may be very well-meaning, and some of them have really *good* advice that you *should* take into consideration. Some of them, however, don't know what the hell they're talking about, and are only projecting their fears of mortality on you as a way of mitigating their own insecurities.

Your true friends will give you the space and patience you need to figure it out yourself (and yes, you are going to have to figure it out yourself). They'll support you and cheer you on as you do, and be just as happy to witness your triumphs as they were heartbroken to witness your tragedies. These people are the kinds of companions you *want* on your journey, and if once in a while they have their head up their ass, forgive them, because they're only human. In their hearts, they just want to see you okay again, and may not know how else to help. The ones you *don't* need in your life are the people who belittle, blame, or dismiss you in the wake of disaster. These people you can kick to the curb and be better without, trust me.

What matters when you start receiving all this advice for self-improvement is, do you know who you are, and can you summon the courage to be that? If you can answer these questions with a *yes* and a *yes,* then you're ready for the next step.

Chapter Five: Easy Street

"She's 22. She's not even out of college!"

A friend of mine was distraught because her boyfriend of seven years had, at 36, broken up with her... and promptly started dating a younger woman. A *much* younger woman.

"I don't understand it! I gave him SEVEN YEARS!"

I understood it. I understood it better than I understood how I can go into Whole Foods for one thing and come out with twelve.

But what do you tell a woman with a broken heart?

Their relationship had been three years of good, followed by four years of on-again-off-again strife. Ultimatums, moving in, moving out. They were always "taking a break" or "getting back together," and it seemed like both of them were trying every recipe they could think of to come up with some magic combination that would make them both happy, without stressing them both out. Ups and downs and setbacks and leaps of faith - it was exhausting just watching, and no one was surprised when they ended it, except her. Truth is, a lot of us were relieved. But here she was, dumbfounded. Aside from the obvious, what could he possibly be getting out of a relationship with a girl ten years younger than her?

At the time, I could never find the words to explain it to my friend, but I think she eventually figured it out. After seven years of sturm and drang, she came to want exactly what her ex wanted: *easy*. Simple. *Uncomplicated*. Appreciative. She finally married a guy who felt lucky to have her, and he wasn't perfect on paper or male model handsome, but she never felt like she had to fight to keep his attention, and after four years of hell, it was *heaven*.

Older men don't date young girls just because they're unwrinkled and perky. My theory is, what men like about younger women is that they're just plain **easier** than older women. And *especially* if a man has gone through a difficult time, who wouldn't want to come home to Easy Street?

Think about it: when a man buys a 22 year-old flowers, takes her on vacations, and does all the things that, at 36, he's already figured out women like, he is **miles** ahead of the 24 year-olds he's competing with. She may have a hot neighbor who looks like Zac Efron, but he's in flip-flops doing a keg stand, too hungover to get his shit together and call her. And here you come rolling up in a crisp shirt with a job and a car that's only three years old? You look like fricking Prince Charming and you're not even *trying*! Your part of the relationship is *easy*, because you already know what to do – there's no pressure to perform because you've been playing this game twice as long. Hell, you know the plays so well, you can half-ass it and still come across as Brad Pitt in *Meet Joe Black*. And how GOOD does that feel after years of going through the trouble of making the effort for someone your own age, who sees your "surprise" bouquet of flowers as a thinly veiled attempt to get laid, or a pathetic bribe to let you go to Vegas with your buddies? How *nice* is it to be around someone for whom all this is new and exciting? Who wants to live on the corner of Unimpressed and Doghouse when you can live on Easy Street?

Now, dating younger women (and men, ladies) is not the only way human beings seek out the *simple* after the *ridiculously difficult*. What is the first thing an accountant does after tax season? A corporate audit? Not unless he's a certified masochist. *He goes on vacation.* He takes it easy.

The problem is, when you've been through something truly gnarly and life-threatening – like the world's worst custody battle, or three kinds of cancer in two years, or a climbing accident that shattered your pelvis in twelve places – it's easy to make a case for an *extended* vacation. You start to tell yourself you *deserve* it, and the next thing you know, you're not just taking a break to get some R & R; you're moving to Margarita-ville and justifying it by telling everyone how *hard* you've had it. Eventually, you decide the smart thing is to *only* date 22-year olds, and break up with them the moment they expect you to start acting like a grown up. You become *that* guy – addicted to uncomplicated women because ten years ago, someone was a little hard on you and now your relationship skills have atrophied. Easy Street is a *slippery slope*, friends.

    You have to grow up sometime. Even if it's your current partner, friends, or family who are making it easy for you to *take it easy* while you're in this post-disaster recovery limbo (by tolerating your bimbo girlfriends, by letting you surf their couch), this isn't Never-Never Land, and you're not Peter Pan. Someday, you're going to wake up, and you're going to be 40, or 50, or 60, and if you don't have a job and a plan for your future, it's going to be too late to get one. This isn't a romantic comedy with Matthew McConaughey; this is your *life*, and eventually, everyone is going to be done making it easy for you – even the 20 year-olds. Read this again: **it doesn't matter how hard it's been for you; you are going to have to grow up, and soon.** There's no getting around it – even if you've had a serious illness, or an unplanned pregnancy, or Hurricane Katrina took your house. *You don't get a pass.* Call it whatever you want – manning up, becoming an adult, maturing – every human being on this planet has to do it, including you, whether you like it or not.

    This is why Easy Street doesn't always look like dating a grad student. Sometimes it looks like moving back in with your parents after you get a divorce, or working at a sporting goods store after being laid off, or staying in a relationship that doesn't challenge you. Your mom is doing your laundry. Your job is so mind-numbingly easy, a monkey could do it. You're in a relationship that doesn't require you to take one step out of your comfort zone. In the beginning, all these things are a relief – *thank GOD*, you think. *Thank GOD after so much, I don't have to work so **hard** all the time.* One of my friends, after finishing treatment for cancer, moved to Disney World because, she said, *"I just wanted to be in the Happiest Place on Earth."*

And after surviving something terrible and difficult, most of us **need** a time and place to recoup. *To heal, to feel good again, to rest and recover.* And that's **fine**. Sometimes, Easy Street is **exactly** what you need post-disaster.

But you can't live there forever.

I'll say it again: **You. Can't. Live. There. Forever.**

Eventually, you have to come home, and that means leaving Never Never Land and growing up, just like Wendy and John and Michael.

My advice is this: go ahead and live on Easy Street for a while, but no longer than a year, two max. Then, start packing, and start challenging yourself, a little at a time. Start looking for a job, an apartment, a relationship (because, sometimes Easy Street looks like not getting involved with *anyone*). Start going out of your comfort zone, scaring yourself a little. Let Easy Street be the **bridge** back to the real world, and never forget what it is: *a transition.* Not a *destination.*

"Why *not* live on Easy Street?" You may ask. "Who wants to constantly struggle? *Don't I deserve **easy** after how **hard** I've had it?*"

(There's that sense of entitlement again. Hear it?)

I'll tell you why: because human beings are learning organisms, that's why. **Without development, we atrophy.** Complacency and apathy are not *living*, and we can only be productive members of society if we are living, contributing creatures.

What kind of world would we live in if no one ever grew up? Who would run the power plants and fly the Medivacs and engineer the bullet trains? Human beings don't really *enjoy* purposeless existences. We like to play; we like recreation, but don't confuse this with perpetual irresponsibility. Everyone feels more fulfilled when they feel like they are making contributions to the world that are valued; having a sense of purpose is always better for one's

48

self-esteem than feeling useless. This is why we go to work. Otherwise, everyone would just quit their job and figure out a way to live off public assistance. Even people who hate their jobs show up to them every day because it enables them to feed their self-esteem – by living an independent life, by being a responsible parent, or funding a recreational activity they love.

When you stay too long on Easy Street, it erodes your sense of purpose. You get used to just getting by. You forget what it feels like for your life or your work to *mean something*, and then, you are just an eating, breathing meat suit. Life isn't as hard, but it's not as enjoyable either, because you never get to feel the exhilaration of accomplishment, the victory of your own persistence beating back your self-doubt. Sure, Easy Street is a relief at first, but if you grow too accustomed to it, you eventually fear leaving it, because that means rebuilding muscles you haven't had to use in months. It means getting up off the couch, Mr. Potato-Ass, and putting on your running shoes. It means everything being *hard* again, and you remember what *that* was like, don't you? Being broke, being broken-hearted, being rejected. Why go through that again when you can just stay on Easy Street? *Victory-schmictory*, you might say, *I'll take apathy*.

I'll say it just once: **That's your choice.** You have every right to not take the path less traveled. It's your life. *But,* if you *want* to get home – if you *want* to come back to where you started, and stronger, with a sense of purpose, and an appreciation of the gift that *surviving* truly is – then read on, because I truly believe that your life will be fuller, richer, and more valuable to you if you challenge yourself to *really live it*.

To build strength, you must work a muscle until it fails – until it FAILS. You must *literally tear the fibers until they break*. Then, your body uses what you put into it to rebuild that muscle, making it stronger, and capable of bearing an even greater weight. You can only build resilience and strength by allowing yourself to be broken down (is that a beautiful, perfect design, or what?).

Your emotional muscles work the same way. We must challenge ourselves, pushing past our own comfort zones, to grow. And that means failing, which is scary. Who wants to be scared? No wonder we choose easy. Overcoming the fear of failure simply means learning to trust yourself. Trust your body and your heart and your mind. You are a learning organism and you are DESIGNED for resilience. In fact, *you are designed to come back **stronger** after failure.* But if you never push yourself, if you never challenge yourself for fear of failing again, of losing or being vulnerable again, you will never give yourself the chance to grow or develop. Adversity enables recovery, and recovery enables development. Let it be your greatest teacher, and you will surprise yourself.

Risk, and if you fail, trust that you can recover. I guarantee you will come back stronger.

Chapter Six: The Ricky Bobby Factor

When I was getting ready to finish chemo, I scheduled a job interview with a recruiter. I was 36, had a Green MBA and a diverse resume - four years of managing commercial properties, a year grant writing for a non-profit and developing an environmental internship program, two years of running my own businesses - one online and one in my backyard, literally. I had even written a Youth-Driven Green Plan for the City of Richmond - something no one *on the planet* has done. Still, I had been having trouble finding work, and thought I'd better bite the bullet and call in some reinforcements.

The meeting did not go well. She was late, hadn't reviewed my resume, asked if I had been looking on craigslist and other "Green" job boards - all of which I was familiar with (did I mention I have an MBA?). She suggested that my trouble was probably due to being out of California for a year, and that I might want to volunteer somewhere locally, to add experience to my resume. *Experience to my resume?* I wanted to say. *I have a degree that less than 500 people in the world have, in the fastest growing field there is, and you want me to volunteer somewhere?*

When I spoke to a friend about the meeting, who recruits in a different industry, he dismissed my conclusion that the woman was a moron. "April," he said, "I Googled you." Yeah, so? 30,000 hits on my YouTube Channel, a blog with tons of entries on how to survive a tough economy, how to green your business, ways to cultivate resilience. Who wouldn't want to hire me? "Honey," he said gently, "you had *cancer.* Why would I hire a 36-year old woman who changes jobs every year, especially one with a history of life-threatening disease?" *But that's illegal*, I said, shell-shocked. "Nope," he said. "It's not illegal if you never get an interview."

All of a sudden, everything I'd done in the last ten years seemed like a huge liability. By taking the road less traveled by, by sharing my cancer struggles and triumphs with the world, by making my very name into a BRAND, I had totally screwed myself.

A few days after my meeting with the recruiter, I was visiting a locally-owned chain of discounted sporting good stores to get a new pair of running shoes. Everyone was so nice, and the store had such a pleasant atmosphere. "I should work *here*," I thought. I filled out an application on a whim, and, two weeks after my chemo was over, they hired me. They hired me even though I wore a baseball cap to work for two months, even though I wasn't done with my treatment (I still had 28 radiation treatments, which had been delayed by another surgery). They even gave me health insurance, despite the fact that I was a cancer survivor, and my coworkers made me laugh and inspired me to get fitter and healthier. For six months, I was on Easy Street – happy every single time I came to work. I started to joke that I felt like the girl who has a "broke-ass" boyfriend she is crazy in love with, who keeps coming back despite the fact that she knows it can't go anywhere.

When I finished treatment, though, things changed. The holiday shopping season came, and with it, reductions in staff but twice as much work. I applied for a promotion, but it went to someone else. I gave them a proposal to green all their stores, at a higher salary, and was told they were only interested in projects that didn't take any extra time or cost any extra money (I wanted to say, "*Well, if I could do THAT, I'd be working for the U.N.*"). The opportunities to "move up quickly" that were referenced when I was hired never materialized, and my two favorite coworkers reduced their hours and eventually quit. I was trying to stay for a year so I could keep my discount, but work was getting more and more frustrating and less and less enjoyable. I found myself wanting to stay at home and work on my book, blog, and videos, rather than drag myself to my "real" job. What happened to the place I couldn't wait to go to in the morning?

If you've seen *Talladega Nights: The Ballad of Ricky Bobby*, you know the story. If you haven't, here it is: Ricky Bobby is a race car driver who is cocky and arrogant. While trying to beat a competitor, he pushes himself too far and gets in a terrible wreck that shakes both his confidence and the confidence of his sponsors. His wife and best friend abandon him, and, broke and alone, he is reduced to living with his mother and delivering pizza on a bike. Ricky Bobby's estranged father, seeking to rebuild his son's confidence, comes back into his life and pushes him to regain his confidence by learning to *"drive with the fear"* that debilitated his career, using unorthodox training like putting a live cougar in the car with him. Even when he can drive again, Ricky Bobby remains unsure of himself, telling his former assistant, Susan, that he has put racing professionally behind him. In an impassioned speech, Susan tells him he must be the man he was born to be, and Ricky Bobby returns to the racetrack. In the end, he triumphs by refusing to give up, and committing to being the best version of himself – someone stronger and more courageous than the man he was before.

Looking back at my frustration with my job, I realized, *I was Ricky Bobby*. I had been an entrepreneur – an adventurer who had jumped off a huge cliff, into an island in the middle of the Pacific, with big dreams of making a difference and changing the world.... and here I was, a year later, delivering pizza. Now, there's nothing wrong with delivering pizza - it's an honest job, and thousands of people do it every day and feed their families doing it. Working at a sporting goods store was, like Ricky Bobby's job, *a safe choice in a world that had become very scary*. At the time, I needed something reliable, dependable, and not too challenging. In other words, *Easy Street*. The last thing I needed after cancer was something that would present me with obstacles and fears that would make me feel insecure about my future. I just needed to be in a place where I felt comfortable, and people I could laugh with every day, *because I had just been through six months of chemotherapy.* The real challenge came once my treatment was over - once I didn't have to worry about getting sick again – because being in a place where my potential was never going to be tapped, let alone maximized, felt like a waste of my time, and I could barely stand it.

I once asked a friend of mine, who is a professional kayaker, if he knew any guys who went down a rapid the wrong way and almost died... then never paddled anything above a Class III again. "Oh, yeah," he said. "Definitely." How many people do you know, who have had their heart broken and vow to never love again? One of my best friends has been terribly disappointed by love twice, and yet, she is in a wonderful relationship that challenges her every day to have faith in love again. Every day she is still with her boyfriend is, in a small way, an affirmation - that this time won't necessarily be like the last. It takes a tremendous amount of faith and hope to go out on a limb again - believe me, I know - but if you want to survive, you cannot live a constricted life, for fear of it falling apart again. It's akin to depriving your body of oxygen, because you don't want to take a deep breath again. But we have to breathe, and breathe deep, if we want to truly live.

My solution for what I call "the Ricky Bobby Factor" is the same as the movie's - you have to do what you love, even if that means (ESPECIALLY if that means) learning to *"drive with the fear."* And yes, you will probably have to get in the car with a cougar. Not a "real live cougar," of course - but something that really and truly scares the crap out of you. It's the only way to hit your "RESET" button - and that button is the key to reclaiming your courage and hope.

What I did - albeit unintentionally - was go on a climbing trip with First Descents (http://www.firstdescents.org). "FD" started as a kayaking camp, which I think is a perfect metaphor for life after cancer (or any other disaster). When you are kayaking, you are floating on an uncontrollable, unpredictable force of nature - just like life. You cannot control a river - it is going to twist and turn and there is nothing you can do about it but learn to ride the waves - to practice being unafraid of the rises and dips on the ride. You can learn to navigate, to paddle, to float, to rest, and all these skills will make the ride easier and more enjoyable, but once you are in the river, *you are in the river*, and there is no getting out. When I was climbing with FD, the greatest lesson I learned is that your footing - your grip on the wall - is always more certain than you think. I would take a step and think, "That little crack is not going to hold my weight!" and miraculously, it would. I learned to trust my body, trust my instincts, and have faith in myself. After just a week with First Descents, I felt like I had come back home to myself. I realized that it was because for the first time in months, I had actually BEEN myself - a climber, a dreamer, an adventurer who took big leaps of faith and hung on for dear life when the ride got scary. I laughed, looking in the mirror when I got home, because I finally recognized the person staring back.

It's easy, after disaster, to put your potential in a box, and vow to never dream again. It makes life so much easier, doesn't it? Not having dreams, not going out on limbs. You can tell yourself, like Ricky Bobby, that the racetrack's not for you anymore, that you can be happy *without* the thrill of victory, because it means never having to suffer the tragedy of defeat.

The danger of resigning yourself to a less-challenging life is simple: the heart wants what the heart wants. The same instinct that fought for your survival fought for the very thing you deny yourself when you give up your passions. Why else would you want to go on living, except to make the dreams of your heart a reality? We live on this earth to suck the marrow out of life, and trust me, your heart knows it. Lying to yourself about that not being an option anymore will *kill your spirit*, and when that goes, your will to live will inevitably follow.

Crucial to the process of coming home is not giving up on yourself. Do not use the fact that you have fallen down destroy your dreams of scaling new heights again. Recovery does not mean never letting yourself be the person you dreamed of being, of resigning yourself to a life without racecars. Don't talk yourself into believing that following your dreams was why everything blew up in your face. Don't live a half-life by giving up now. You made it through the woods. You'll make it home by summoning the courage to rebuild everything, including your dreams.

Chapter Seven: Check In, or Check Out?

In the first part of this book, I talked about the three stages you must go through on the road to survivorship. You must give up the future you thought you had, acknowledge your mortality, and recognize that you have a decision to make: to be, or not to be.

In this second part, we've talked about the ways we half-live. You may have decided that you want to live, but the life you've committed to may be a half-life – one where you aren't being yourself, one that doesn't challenge you, or one that abandons the dreams you had before everything fell apart.

Before we take the next step, into the last stage of survivorship, where you craft your "new normal," I'm going to ask you one question: do you want to check in, or do you want to check out?

The story you tell yourself, not only about what happened to you, but about the future you can expect in this life, is going to be crucially important at this stage of your survivorship. In the weeks and months and years ahead of you, there will be times when you will go back to this moment, when you decided to check in or check out, and you *will* question your decision, even if briefly. So take this moment to really think about if you're ready to check in, and what level of commitment you're willing to bring to that decision.

This is the part where you have to ask, *do I **want** to suffer the slings and arrows of outrageous fortune*? Because I'm not going to lie to you: there is simply no way to avoid them if you are going to live here on earth. Money won't make them go away; love won't make them go away. Life is full of ups and downs and challenges and disappointments, and as long as you're alive, you're going to have to deal with slings and arrows.

You *do* have a choice – the only choice, really, that we have – and it's an important one. **You don't have to be here**.

Now, most people don't like to think about their mortality, but you know, if you are just done with the challenge that life is – and is going to be, as long as you're alive – you can hang up your hat right now and check out for good and never have to be disappointed or hurt ever again. It might break a lot of hearts for you to give up, but it's still your choice to make, however painful it may be to everyone else.

Let me tell you something about cancer: cancer is an easy friggin' way to check out. No one will blame you - they'll blame the disease, or the doctors, or the treatments. And you know what? It takes a lot of frigging courage to NOT check out when cancer comes in and wrecks your life like a bunch of B-12s over Dresden.

I've heard survivors say, "Why is everyone calling me *brave* just for taking my medicine? I don't *feel* brave; I feel like shit." People say things like this because it IS brave, to *choose to* keep suffering the slings and arrows. To keep going into a room, to keep putting an IV in your chest, when you know it's going to make you feel like crap, knowing that your future might not necessarily be easier or happier because of it. That *is* fucking brave – it is the very **definition** of courage, to persist in the face of adversity, with nothing but a shred of hope that it will not always be this bad, that it might be worth it to fight for more time on this earth. It's nothing short of **brave** to keep living, when it would be easier to die.

Every day, I make a choice to check in, and I'll be honest - it's not always easy. There are still days when I want to check out – when I just have one disappointment too many in a 24-hour period. But there are strategies I have in place that serve as a kind of safety net, to remind me why I went through chemo. The biggest of these is returning to the moment when I decided that my life was worth sticking around for. I looked into my heart, and told myself, *I don't know what my future will hold, and if it holds something wonderful, and amazing, and worth looking forward to, I will miss out on that if I choose to check out.*

Even if that's the only story you tell yourself to make it through a tough night, or a tough week, or a tough year, if it keeps you waking up in the morning, **that's all you need to stay alive long enough to get to a place where it will be easier to hang on**.

So right now, the most important decision you can make is this: *do you want to check in, or do you want to check out?*

If you want to check out, the rest of this book is irrelevant. Godspeed.

If you want to check in, then keep reading, and I'll show you how.

PART THREE: CHECKING IN

I spoke with a woman halfway through chemo whose best friend was fighting the same cancer I had. It had spread to her friend's bones, then her liver, then her brain, and she was looking for an oncologist who specialized in liver cancer. The woman was distraught at the thought of someone so close to her having months to live. "I'm just trying to do everything I can to help her," she said, on the verge of tears. I asked if her friend had thought of changing her diet. "We can't even get her to stop smoking!" she said, exasperated. I thought, but didn't say, *then I'm sorry to be the one to tell you, but your friend wants to die.*

In this last part of this book, I'm going to make you fight for your life. It's not going to get handed to you on a silver platter, and on the road ahead, you may actually feel like there are forces working to keep it from you. People you love will tell you that you *can't have* the life you want, or imply that you're crazy for even trying to build it (trust me, if you build it, it *will* come). Setbacks and unforeseen disappointments are going to make you question your resolve. You're going to be tempted to quit, and you're probably going to give up once or twice.

That is *okay*.

What matters, as the old adage goes, is not how many times you fall down, but how many times you get back up. This section of the book is about how to get back up. We're going to talk about the things that will knock you down and ways to not *stay* down. I'm not going to give you ways to get back up that only work if you're rich, or beautiful, or lucky. These are the strategies that worked for me when I was hanging on to a shred of hope so small, it felt like the only thing that was keeping my heart beating. The only caveat is, I can't give you my will to live. I can't do the work for you. YOU have to cultivate your survival instinct. YOU have to use these strategies like a four-star General on a mission. This is war, and you are fighting for your life, so if an air raid doesn't work, you bring in the tanks, and if the tanks don't work, you call in the troops, and if the troops don't work, then you need to call up NORAD and order some missiles, because if you lose this battle, it's over and there's no coming back. If you win though – *when* you win – you will find yourself safe at home, and life's lemons will have very little chance of disrupting your peace of mind.

Key to getting the most out of these chapters is your attitude. None of any of this will work if you have not committed to everything that has come before them. By now, you have to have accepted that the life you thought you were going to have is gone. You have to believe that this life – this window – is all you get, and there's no going back. You have to *want* to live. In addition, you have to be committed to living *your* life – not someone else's – and to living that life fully, which includes not giving up on your dreams. If you can say all this about where you are right now, then you're ready to check in, and I can help you fight for your future.

Chapter Eight: Traveling Light

It's important to remember, once you've made the decision to check in, to "get busy living," that this doesn't automatically predispose you to a life where you start getting everything you want. *Never forget that few things in life are certain.* Even quantum mechanics proposes the minutest possibility of the impossible happening, and while we manage our sanity by hedging our bets, I believe the key to long-term contentment is simply getting really good at rolling with the punches.

Crucial to this is **curbing your sense of entitlement.**

Now, you might say, "Entitlement? I don't have a sense of entitlement!" But… I'm here to say that, yes, you do. **You absolutely do.** The good news is, who can blame you? We live in a world *designed to cultivate* a sense of entitlement. Whether it's because you subscribe to a dogma that reinforces a belief that the Creator of the Universe favors you, or because you're surrounded by television ads and billboards proclaiming, "You're Worth It!" the result is the same: human beings (at least those of us in industrialized nations) tend to harbor a kind of low-grade sense of entitlement to a privileged existence.

The irony is, whether we actually *live* a privileged existence is irrelevant; this sense of us *deserving it* is what screws up our contentment. The fact is, you *don't* have a right to a privileged existence, and *believing* that you do will only invite suffering when your expectations are not met.

This chapter is called *Traveling Light* because that's what I want you to start doing: dropping that sense of entitlement, because it's going to be your heaviest burden on this journey home.

So how does one fight this built-in expectation of the world owing us for our troubles? Should human beings just never expect anything? Well, to a certain extent, *yes*.

Let me explain. There is a *balance* between **being hopeful** and **having expectations**, and the difference is a belief: that you *deserve* something. Hope says, "I wish this" but an expectation says, "I am *owed* this." If you practice detachment (which Buddhists tend to be really good at, incidentally) by reminding yourself that 1) the world doesn't owe you anything and 2) you can't control the future, then you'll have a solid advantage in this "minefield of entitlement." Make it a habit to *practice detached desire* – allowing yourself to want things, but not convincing yourself that you are *owed* them by the Universe (or anyone else, for that matter). This will allow you to still clarify your intention and purpose in life, but not carry the weight of an expectation that might not be met.

"But HOW can I want something without inevitably *expecting* to GET it?" you might ask. My answer: *exactly*. **Exactly.** So travel light, my friends – leave your expectations behind you.

Now, the second part of this chapter has to do with leaving something *else* behind: the **pain** we carry around as a result of unmet expectations. You see, it's easy to be *angry* when you don't get what you want, but more often than not, we're **hurt**. Instead of feeling cheated, we feel *slighted*. Punished. And then, we beat ourselves up for having the *audacity* to hope, the *arrogance* to wish and want and dream. We shake our heads, telling ourselves, "I **never** should have reached so high! What made me think I actually **deserved** to be happy?!" AH! See? There's the rub.

It's not about what you deserve. Let me say that again: *It's not about what you deserve.* You've been telling yourself a story, about how the world is a place built on cause and effect, and if you take an action, life will serve up what you want. But *that's just not how it works*. Bad things happen, for no reason at all. Bears stumble into campgrounds and maul toddlers. Vegetarians get cancer and leave widowers. Tornadoes destroy high schools and hospitals.

I know this is hard to take, so if you want to tell yourself a different story that makes you feel better, go right ahead. I tell *myself* a story, that the hardships I'm faced with in life are pre-destined by a divine Creator, designed to build my character, so I can share what I learn with others and become a stronger, more appreciative human being because of the experience. And you know what? Telling myself this story makes me feel not so alone in the Universe, and not so put-upon by circumstance. It may be true, it may not, but if it keeps me happy and it's not hurting anyone, does it matter?

Of course I have my moments of, *"How on earth could I think this was going to work out?"* chagrin, but I recognize them for what they are: fear of failure. Risk management. How else to we stave off disappointment except by blaming **ourselves** when things don't turn out as expected? The flip side of carrying a sense of entitlement is saying to ourselves, "I never should have dreamed; I don't deserve it." Instead, we should be saying, "You know, if I'm really honest with myself, I can acknowledge that failure and disappointment was a possibility here, because I had expectations going into it. If I had been open to that possibility, instead of convincing myself there was no way everything wouldn't turn out perfect, I would probably feel a lot better about what happened."

Of course you should dream. Dream big! Dream high! Dream far! But check your ego and your sense of entitlement. **The world doesn't owe you a thing.** Attachment and disappointment only threaten contentment when you say, 'I *should* have it.' Hope with all the optimism and positivity you can muster, but also, tell yourself THIS story: *that if it is meant to be, it will be, and if it isn't, it won't.* This is how detachment serves happiness: by freeing us from expectation.

The most damaging thing about a sense of entitlement is how it wears out hope. We build things up: we pile all our happiness onto something - a wedding, a baby, a job. And when we are stood up at the altar, when we have a stillborn child, when we are betrayed by our coworkers and employers, it breaks us in two, but more importantly, *it makes us question our own optimism by eroding hope.* Don't confuse hope with expectation. Hope is a kind of faith that, if desire is untainted by ego, tells us our happiness will be manifested somehow, some way. Emily Dickinson said, *"Hope is the thing with feathers, that perches in the soul, that sings the tune without the words, and never stops at all."* **Expectation**, on the other hand, is hope's controlling brother - its tyrant. Expectation carries with it a sense of obligation, of debts owed, of dues paid and righteousness earned. Hope says, "I wish it"; Expectation says, "I **deserve** it." Recognizing the difference means letting go of the idea that the world functions on a cause-and-effect basis, where payment is rendered and God (or the Universe, or our future spouse, or our unborn children) "owes" us something in return. Let go of your sense of entitlement, and you will cut your disappointment in half (at the very least!).

Chapter Nine: The Hourglass

One of my favorite scenes in all film history is in the *Wizard of Oz*. Dorothy has been captured by the Wicked Witch of the West, and sits trapped her tower. The Witch, unable to remove Dorothy's ruby slippers, thrusts an hourglass in front of her and flips it upside down. *"Do you see that?"* she says to a terrified Dorothy, *"That's how much longer you've got to be alive! And it isn't long, my pretty! It isn't long!"*

When I was first diagnosed with cancer, I didn't feel like I was in danger of dying. I felt like my life was starting to unravel, of course – I could see that I would not be able to farm cacao on Kaua'i, that I was going to have to put a tourniquet on my small business (which was, truthfully, already on life support), and that I would have to sell my house and move back to California. But I was relatively young and still pretty strong. Physically, I never felt like I was in real danger.

That is, until my first chemo.

Chemo sucks. I hear stories of cancer survivors who are like, "Oh, chemo was a breeze; I never missed a day of work!" and I want to say, "What chemo did YOU have?" because mine kicked my ass. I would get tired just mopping my kitchen. Everything I ate gave me horrible indigestion that eventually led to an inflamed gallbladder. I had done triathlons and 30-mile bike rides, but after a month on Adriamycin and Cytoxan, I could barely walk a mile without getting winded. For the first time in my life, I didn't feel invincible and ready to take on the world. I felt like I was fighting, every day, and winning, but not without using up every ounce of strength I had.

What really shook my foundations, though, was my first conversation with my California oncologist. "With triple negative cases like yours," Dr. Kuan was saying, "I like to recommend clinical trials, because there isn't a drug you can take after chemo and radiation to keep your cancer from coming back." I looked at her blankly. *To keep it from coming back?* It had never even occurred to me that my cancer could **come back**. I'd had two surgeries to cut it out; I was dumping petrochemicals into my body (despite my green values) to kill any remaining cells. When chemo was over, I was going to shoot radioactive isotopes into my chest. Why on earth would my cancer *come back*? For the first time since my diagnosis, I realized I should be doing everything I possibly can to survive. If not, I was in danger of only surviving *this round*. My mortality suddenly came into crystal clear focus. *Shit*, I thought, *this is it. This is it.*

Some people, when they realize that **this is it**, look at what's left of their life and say to themselves, *"You know, I've painted myself into a corner, and it's never going to get better than this."* And they check out. It might take months; it might take years, but they spend the rest of this little parentheses we have here on earth throwing away the minutes they have left. If you're reading this chapter, I hope it means that's not you. If you're reading this chapter, I hope it means that you've decided that, despite life not turning out the way you thought it was going to, your future is *worth* checking in for. And if you *have* made the decision to live, and you *know* that the life you have left is an hourglass, then what do you want the next 100 years to be? This is where the hard work begins, because you have to dream again. You have to stop whining about how you almost didn't make it, and start crafting a post-disaster life that embraces and acknowledges and honors your survivorship. You must ask yourself: how do I want to spend the years I have left, be it 5 or 50?

Now, it's not going to be easy, to craft a life worth living for. It's going to be frigging hard work. But let me tell you: if you do, you'll never get to the end of your life and, as Thoreau once said, *discover that you did not live.* You will know that you can build a life that is not only worth living for, but worth looking forward to, no matter what the future holds.

When I was in my late twenties, all my friends were turning 30. They were whining about getting old, about 30 being some deadline for the end of their youth (it seems so ridiculous, looking back, now that I'm 37). At 27, I had taken up running again and was training for my first marathon, and one of my tenants was training for an Ironman - an insane triathlon that started with a 2.4-mile swim, followed with a 112-mile bike ride, and finished with a 26.2 mile run. She suggested I try a sprint distance triathlon (750 m swim, 20 km bike, 5 km run), and at first I dismissed the idea as crazy. A week later, though, I found myself imagining what it would be like to do something that I thought might be outside my realm of capability.

We all have ideas about what we think we're capable of. We tell ourselves stories, or believe the stories other people tell us, about the things we can and can't do, so when Nicole suggested that it was *possible* for someone like me to do even the shortest of triathlons, it was like a tiny crack suddenly formed in my head. *She thinks I can do a triathlon?* "You just ran ten miles last weekend, didn't you?" she asked, and I could feel the crack getting bigger. *Yes, but...* "You know, if you can workout for two hours, you can totally do a triathlon." And you know what I did then? *I believed her.* It was that simple. And the next thing I knew, my assumptions about what I could and couldn't do began to crumble. *What else can I do?* I thought.

Well, I did the tri, and the marathon, and two other events that year, and on my 28th birthday, I thought, "You know, I don't want to hit 30 and be moaning and groaning about what I *can't* do anymore. I want to start my 30s celebrating what I CAN do!" I figured if I ran a 5K every four weeks for the next two years, I could do 26 by my 30th birthday. Added to my 4, that was "30-by-30" - an accomplishment that would not only make turning 30 worth celebrating, it would make turning 30 something worth *looking forward* to.

Over the next two years, the 5Ks were replaced by other triathlons, trail runs I had never done before, and bike rides in towns I had never been to. I did the Providian Relay three times in a row, the Big Sur Half Marathon, and a Muddy Buddy. I had so much fun in the last two years before I turned 30 that when my 30th birthday finally came, I rang it in like New Year's.

Now, I know I'm only 37, but if there's anything I've learned in my time here thus far, it's that there are only two paths in life: enjoying it, or not enjoying it. As Robert Frost says in *The Road Not Taken*, the paths look "really about the same" – there will be slings and arrows on both, regardless. What differs is your **perception** – and the story you tell yourself – about the path you walked. "Somewhere ages and ages hence," as Frost says, you will be thinking of the path you took, and wondering if it should have been different, *could* have been different. Crafting a life worth living starts with taking a moment to imagine that future place and time, and asking yourself, "What will I want to remember about my life, when I look back on it?"

When I first Googled survivor statistics for Stage 3 Triple Negative Breast Cancer, everything I read said I had a 67% chance of still being alive 5 years after my diagnosis. I did the math and realized that would be when I was 39 - about a week before my 40th birthday, in fact. While most women dread turning 40, I am really looking forward to it, because if I make it to 40, the odds of me living cancer-free for the rest of my life skyrocket - I become part of the general population, with no more risk of getting cancer than anyone else. Talk about a life worth looking forward to.

Lots of people live their whole lives just waiting to retire, so they can "get busy living." My dad used to talk all the time about what he was going to do when he retired: he wanted to move to Reno, into the house he and my grandparents owned, so they could live with him. He wanted to teach kindergarten at the school across the street, and buy a red Corvette, and plant roses all around the house. He said my sister and I could come visit and stay in the guest room, and we could go skiing anytime we wanted. It wasn't that my father hated his life or his job - he never struck me as an unhappy man, even though I know he must have struggled. It was just that he had all these dreams he was saving for later, that couldn't come true until he retired.

My father never got to make any of those dreams come true. He died at 53, of a heart condition he didn't know he had. My grandparents sold the house in Reno and my grandmother died five years later. I didn't go skiing for ten years after my dad died - it was something we always did as a family, and I think a part of me just didn't enjoy it without him. When I finally got back on the slopes, I was just as good a skier, but it wasn't the same.

Why do we save our happiness for later? Why do we put off joy?

I call the last stage of survivorship The Yellow Wood, because this is where your path will diverge. *Don't think about what you can't do because of what you don't have.* For once in your life, make a list - not a list of the things you couldn't live without, but of the things you couldn't die without - things you can't bear to miss out on.

When I came back from my First Descents trip, I made a list - a "40-by-40" - forty things I wanted to be able to say I had done, if I found myself in the 33% that wouldn't make it to 5 years without a recurrence. It's not that I don't think I will make it; it's just that now, *I'm acutely aware of the hourglass that life is.* I don't kid myself that there will always be a "later," because the fact is, our time here is limited. "Live like you're dying?" Newsflash: *we're all dying. No one here gets out alive, remember?*

This "40-by-40" list, as simple as it sounds, is just something to keep me going, milestone by milestone, reminding me of the reason why I want to be here - to live the life I fought cancer for (and won). If you want to revel in your survivorship, make your own list. It doesn't matter if it's a Top Ten, a thousand places to see before you die, or a score you want to beat on a video game. Set a goal for something that you *almost* think you can't do, and use it to rebuild your hope about the future (and remember, you have to be somewhat realistic here - not everyone can walk on the moon just because they beat cancer, and setting an unrealistic goal is just a cop-out disguised as a "big dream").

Remember those men leading lives of quiet desperation? Don't be one. Don't give up on your dreams and don't save them for later. Don't be afraid to take the path less traveled by - it will make all the difference.

Chapter Ten: Dreams With Deadlines

Okay, so now you're all amped up. You're ready to Get Busy Living and write the Bucket List to end all Bucket Lists, right? Well…. Not *quite* yet, my friend. First, a lesson in *survivorship* goal setting.

But wait, you say – I know all about "Goal Setting." Goals must be S.M.A.R.T. – Specific, Measurable, Attainable, Realistic (or, some say, Relevant), and Timely – that's all there is to it. Right? Anyone who's ever been forced to sit in a corporate goal-setting class knows this.

Nope.

We're not talking about hitting your monthly sales targets here. We're not talking about losing ten pounds or cleaning out the garage. This is your *life* we're talking about. You need not just a goal, but a *process* that will inspire you to go on living when you're suffering those slings and arrows and you don't think you can hang on anymore. The kind of goal setting you're going to do now is in a whole different class by itself, because it has to be able to get you home when you want to sit down and give up.

When I was 12, I got a D in Pre-Algebra. My father, an immigrant from the Philippines, worked his whole life to give me opportunities he never had growing up, and when he saw that D on my report card, he sat me down at the dining room table for a *talk*. I was terrified.

"So… do you want to work at McDonalds?" he asked me.

"No," I said, in the shaky voice of a pre-teen who knows she's in big trouble.

"Because at 18, you're out of my house, and with grades like this… you're going to work at McDonalds. Now, it's an honest job, but… you know, it's hard to pay the rent on minimum wage. So, I'm going to ask you *one more time*, do you **want** to work at McDonalds?"

I shook my head vigorously, still unsure of where, exactly, he was going with this. He nodded, putting my report card aside.

"Okay, then. Go upstairs, and put on your running shoes."

"What?"

"*Go upstairs and put on your running shoes.* You need to learn some discipline, so you're coming running with me **every day** until you get these grades back up."

And with that began six years of running with my father, every day, rain or shine. My grades improved by the next quarter, of course, but I kept running with him, and to this day credit him with cultivating within me not only a sense of discipline, but endurance, stamina, and – thanks, Dad – double-barreled calf muscles. Even though I'm not a very fast runner – I can do maybe a 12-minute mile on a good day, 10 minutes on a track if I try really hard – I love it all the same. I love it because running is something just about anyone can do. It doesn't require any particular skill or talent, and if you keep at it, you just get better.

Now, don't worry – I'm not going to tell you that the first lesson in our goal-setting process is becoming a runner. What running did for me was exactly what my father hoped it would – it taught me **discipline**, which I define as *the practice of maintaining a sustainable pace to get from one destination to another*. **Cultivating discipline is the key to survivorship goal-setting,** and the beautiful thing is, you don't have to be a runner to do it.

Of course, if you've ever dedicated yourself to anything that requires skill-building (and believe me, getting home after surviving a disaster is going to give you an opportunity for some SERIOUS skill-building), you'll already have an understanding of the commitment and effort it takes to get better at something. The saying goes, "How do you get to Carnegie Hall?" The answer: "Practice, practice, practice."

Anything you practice at, you will get better at doing, whether it's falling apart, or putting yourself back together. If you practice putting one foot in front of the other, you will get better at that too.

In this chapter, we're going to start small, and ease into goal-setting, because no one becomes an Olympic marathoner overnight. If you apply yourself, however – every day, again and again – whatever you're trying to get better at will get easier and easier. One of my favorite personal trainers once told me the key to change is not being consistent, but being *consistently* consistent. You can't practice something for a while and then stop, or those muscles will atrophy. You have to commit to working on something you can keep working on, even if it seems too easy at first. Don't worry – as you keep at it, you will find yourself setting more and more challenging goals to achieve. For now, though, let's talk about the *qualities* of the goals we want to set.

There are two components to survivorship goal-setting: *inspiration* and *perspiration*. The reason for this is twofold. First, you need an *inspiring* goal because you will have times during this rebuilding process when you are tired or broke or disappointed, and only something that truly inspires you will keep the light in your heart lit bright enough to make you ignore all that and keep going in spite of it. Second, you need a goal that will make you *work* for its achievement, because working your ass off to make something happen not only makes you truly value and appreciate it when it does; it rebuilds your confidence in yourself as you gain *traction*. Traction leads to a sense of *accomplishment*, which will restore your faith in a world where things can be good again (incidentally, as a nice side benefit, sweating for your happiness tends to wear away at any ideas you have in your head that you deserve something for free).

There are no shortcuts in rebuilding your life post-disaster (again, no one becomes a virtuoso overnight) and *lasting* happiness doesn't just fall from the sky. It has to be cultivated, sometimes step by agonizing step. The path to bliss isn't a sprint – it's a marathon – but if you can cultivate the discipline it takes to keep practicing, you can go the distance.

When I was at my lowest point in my cancer treatment – so depressed I almost skipped a chemotherapy session – it was actually *running* that saved my life. I was watching my business shake and falter; my home was on the market for less than I paid for it and still wasn't selling. I had lost my hair, my strength, my hope, and one day, I just reached a point where I didn't think I wanted to live anymore. Death seemed like the easiest way out of all my problems, because the future I thought I was going to have was gone, and I couldn't imagine life getting any better.

Thankfully, I had the sense to know that something wasn't right, and I told my doctor about my struggle to snap out of it. She suggested anti-depressants, which would have taken weeks to work – weeks that, frankly, I just didn't think I had in me. In desperation, I turned to a treadmill. I thought, *"Exercise releases endorphins. Endorphins make you feel better. Maybe if I start running, I can release enough of them to lift this depression."* As ridiculous as it sounds, I figured it was worth a shot, as long as I started out easy and my doctor monitored me.

The next day, I half-walked, half-jogged a mile, and it took me nearly twenty minutes, but I did it, and amazingly, I felt better. I went back the next day, eventually working up to a 4-mile walk. One day in the gym, I saw an old magazine with a pull-out map of the New York Marathon. As I traced the world-famous route with my fingers, I told myself one day I'd have the strength to run it, and a year and a half later, I crossed the finish line in Central Park. That map was tucked in my pocket the whole way, reminding me of how far I'd come – on nothing but inspiration and perspiration (and, okay – a whole lot of discipline).

What made crossing that finish line so sweet was not how far I'd run – it was how far I'd *come*. A truly inspiring goal must take into account where you are now, where you thought you would be, and the value that you attached to that now-gone "future place." When I was half-walking, half-jogging a 20-minute mile, the thought of doing 25 more seemed crazy, but not *that* crazy. I'd done a marathon when I was 27, and I knew I could do it again; I just didn't know how long it would take to build up my stamina. I knew I could get back to Carnegie Hall; I just had to practice. The question was, how long, and how much?

Crucial in survivorship goal-setting is having a realistic understanding of the goal you're trying to accomplish, and an awareness of the discipline and practice it's going to take to achieve it (and believe me, you want a goal that is going to require discipline and practice to achieve). If you've never done something before, it might be a thrilling, exciting prospect to put it on a to-do list, but you're at a slight disadvantage, because you're going to have to rely on other people's experiences and advice to prepare yourself. This is important, because what's going to matter is not whether or not you've done something before, but if you've adequately prepared yourself to undertake it. If you're already thinking of a Bucket List filled with things only Olympians and billionaires can do, you are going to be facing an uphill battle. I'm not saying it's a brick wall, but setting yourself up for failure helps no one, especially you.

Another note: post-crisis is **not** the time to take your chances and jump into the wild blue yonder. You're floundering right now because your life probably had a structure, and now some disaster has not only blown that structure apart, but it's tapped into the lizard part of your brain that knows the world is an unpredictable, uncontrollable place. You're at the bottom of a well, trying to get out, and a wing and a prayer is not going to help you right now. It will only make you feel more at the mercy of an uncontrollable world. Even when I went on a cross-country road trip, I didn't just get in my car and drive – I had a budget and a schedule. What you need right now is a *ladder* – a structured plan that will get you to the top, and that's what you're going to build, one rung at a time. As you do, it will cultivate your discipline, because it's going to take a lot of dedication to build that ladder. When you get tired, or bored, or unmotivated, it will remind you that the only way you're going to get out of this hole is to keep climbing.

Now, to craft this list of goals – each requiring a fair amount of perspiration, and providing a healthy amount of inspiration – you'll need to revisit both the life you had, and the future you *thought* you had.

First, sit down and make a list of everything you've **lost** because of whatever tragedy you've survived. For example, the year I was diagnosed with breast cancer, I lost my hair, my strength, my small business, and my home.

Second, make a list of all the *future* things you're *imagining* you lost – those dreams and accomplishments that are now on a shelf because of whatever happened to you (recognize that some of this will be melodramatic and untrue, but make the list anyway). Go back to a moment when, in the middle of your crisis, you said to yourself, *"Well, I guess I can kiss that dream good-bye..."* and you'll be on the right track. As for me, there were a lot of things on that list, like going to Paris for a chocolate tour with my friend Anne (with so many medical bills, I thought I would never have room in my financial future for such a luxury). Because of the threat of lymphedema in my right arm, I thought I'd never be able to garden again, or hike Kilimanjaro – a dream I'd had for years. Note that although these are the things that were not *technically* taken away from you – because you never had them in the first place – they count all the same, so add them.

Lastly, make a list of all those big life goals you had before this disaster – things that, if you hadn't made it through, you would be sad to not have accomplished. Imagine that you hadn't made it this far, that you weren't that lucky, and you're sitting with St. Peter at the Pearly Gates thinking about everything you missed out on. On that list for me were some funny things – playing a zombie in a movie, seeing the Oprah Winfrey Show with my friend Loren, going skydiving with my friend Ian. Add these things to the list, and don't be afraid to put down silly simple things – they don't have to be grand adventures – it can be as easy as seeing an old friend you used to play volleyball with in junior high, or taking your kid to a Braves game.

You now have a list with three types of things on it – things you lost, things you think you can't have anymore, and things you always wanted. For a moment, ignore the reason why they're on your list, and divide them up into five categories: Things you can accomplish in 1) three months, 2) six months, 3) a year, 4) two years, and 5) five years. I like to say, be optimistic, but also realistic: as I mentioned, is not the time for wings and prayers. You want a ladder, not a pipe dream. This is a list of goals that you can accomplish with discipline and self-determination, not a list of magic wishes you want a genie to grant. It cultivates no discipline (or confidence) to have something handed to you, so if that's what you want, read Chapter Five again.

Look at your list and make sure it is evenly balanced; you want to have about four to ten goals per year, meaning you're looking at a list of 20-50 things you want to achieve over the next five years – some easy, some difficult, but that's okay. Now, *remove anything that doesn't make you happy to think about accomplishing, even things other people want you to accomplish, and especially things that society defines as a barometer of success, but you don't feel motivated to achieve.* Finally, take anything on your list that will take longer than 5 years and move it to another list. Put that list in an envelope and save it for later (like, 5 years from now).

Don't worry about how crazy or unrealistic the things on your list sound just yet. For now, just think about each item on your list, and what it would take in terms of time, money, and other people's help to make happen. Keep in mind, while the world tends to conspire to help you when you put your mind to something, don't expect everything on your list to magically get accomplished. **This is not a list of wishes you want granted.** It's a list of goals that you are going to *make* happen with your own inspiration and perspiration.

Next, put a column next to your list and start brainstorming. If you start to feel discouraged, just imagine you are working for someone else (say, Richard Branson or Jennifer Lopez) and they've hired you to research these goals and develop a timeline and budget for accomplishing each one. Don't think about how *you're* going to accomplish them, just brainstorm about how *someone* would go about accomplishing them.

Now, break each item on your list down into sub-goals or milestones. For example, your five-year goals are probably going to require several sub-goals to accomplish. If you're training for an Ironman, you'll probably have to do a Half-Ironman first, and an Olympic distance triathlon before that. If you're not a swimmer, you'll have to take swimming lessons before that. Get specific on goals that are vague. If one of your goals is visiting a foreign country, think about what kind of climate, food, and infrastructure you are most comfortable in. Can you stay in a rural environment with few facilities? If not, cross third-world countries off your list. Do you speak French? Maybe Paris, Martinique, and Montreal could be options. You've done half the work by putting this list together, but now your task is to create a structure that will not only comfort you, but that's going to *enable* you to accomplish these goals.

Once you've come up with your list, narrowed it down to the goals that really matter to you, and clarified the resources required to accomplish them, you're ready for the next step: building your arsenal.

Chapter Eleven: Building Your Arsenal

By now, I hope you have come to realize a singular truth about life: it has its ups and downs. It's not all up; it's not all down. You will *never* get to a point where everything is *always* good, and it is a waste of what precious little time you have here on earth to attempt to get to this imaginary perfect place, that only exists in Walgreens commercials.

The word *arsenal* originated in the early 16th century, from a word used to describe a dock where ships were repaired. It literally means, "a house where fabrication takes place." What this chapter is about is giving you tools you need to get seaworthy again. These tools will not eliminate suffering from your life, but will enable you bear it without feeling like nothing is ever going to get any better. They aren't magic; they're just simple strategies and practices I use to hang onto my peace of mind when the world threatens to fall apart again. I use them to patch myself up, and get back out to sea.

Tool #1: Stock Your Medicine Cabinet

When I was in Kaua'i, going through my own challenges, I lived with a good friend who worked in mental health. In counseling her clients, she utilized a metaphor that I found incredibly useful. Many of them were on medication for their illnesses, and found the day-to-day struggles that most of us handle very easily – grocery shopping, getting to work, living with family members – extremely challenging. To help them cope, my roommate would advise her clients to imagine they had access to an imaginary "medicine cabinet" that held all of their most effective ways of managing these daily struggles. For those in treatment, of course, some of the things in their medicine cabinet *were* actual medicine, but what she encouraged them to *add* to their cabinet were simple strategies for coping with stress and anxiety. One client might have "talking with my counselor" in his medicine cabinet; another might have "painting," or "listening to music," or "making a list." Her goal was to encourage them to not rely on just *one* coping strategy, because it puts a person in the vulnerable position of having all their eggs in one basket.

I loved the idea of having a "go to" place for a variety of coping strategies, and to this day, am always looking for things that work for me, to put in my own "medicine cabinet" (actually, at this point, I have a medicine *closet*). When life is disappointing, when I struggle, I listen to music, go for a bike ride, get outdoors, or call close friends. Sometimes, I dance, eat ice cream, or take a Midol, or read a bunch of Best of Craigslist ads to make me laugh. I've been known to watch cheesy action movies, flip through *Sunset* magazine, or take a hot bath and a nap. All of these things work for me, and they may work for you; they may not. The point is, when life gets *me* down, I have two dozen kinds of "medicine" to help me get myself back **up**, and none of them are controlled substances (although, Talenti's Salted Caramel Gelato is arguably dangerous in large doses). I have this arsenal because I *consciously and deliberately* **collect** strategies that work for me. Build a medicine cabinet full of coping strategies, and you will never be left facing a tough time, wondering how you are going to make yourself feel better. Got that? *Make **yourself** feel better*. You have to take responsibility for your own happiness.

One important note: when filling *your* medicine cabinet, take a careful look at the coping strategies you turn to in times of trouble. Is your cabinet filled with destructive habits disguised as "solutions" – alcohol, drugs, self-abuse, or talking to unsupportive friends? If so, it's time to balance those out with alternatives – things that encourage and rebuild your spirit. It's understandable for anyone to keep chocolate hazelnut truffles or red wine in their medicine cabinet, but if these are the *only* two coping strategies you use when things get hard, you're putting yourself in the position of becoming an obese alcoholic every time life gives you lemons. Strive for balance in your medicine cabinet. For every destructive habit, come up with at least two healthier alternatives, and gradually weed out the things that set you back by replacing them with things that build you up and move you forward.

Tool #2: Hedge Your Bets

Life is unpredictable and uncontrollable – this, we know – but, there are ways to hedge your bets. Not with everything, of course, but with some things – getting a ride home after a party, for instance – you can hedge your bets: don't let the drunk guy drive. It's not going to guarantee your safety, but it certainly won't hurt your odds of getting home in one piece. Or, if you're cooking, you can throw everything together and cross your fingers, or you can follow a Julia Child recipe. The same goes for life. While we can't control everything, we *can* hedge our bets a little by building what I call "opportunities for happiness" into our schedules.

Now, I'm not talking about creating wild, crazy expectations here. Building opportunities for happiness doesn't mean clearing your schedule for a June wedding just because your New Year's Eve blind date went well. That's just setting yourself up for a major unmet expectation. I'm talking about going into your medicine cabinet, picking out the things that make you happy, and making room for them on your calendar so that you don't end up going weeks at a time without a little levity in your life.

In 2010, I looked ahead to 2011 and surmised that it *might* be kind of a difficult year. I was planning on relocating to another state, jobhunting, probably declaring bankruptcy, and fighting my health insurance company in a lawsuit. I was also facing not *having* health insurance, and going on the third year of my clinical trial. Thankfully, I had a lot of things going for me: I had some savings to get me by, a ton of airline miles, a place to live with my aunt and uncle, and I'd just won a six-week lease of a brand-new car (with gas included).

I looked at all my assets, then looked at my 40-by-40 list, and came up with a three-month schedule filled with hard work – jobhunting, writing, and meeting the requirements of the car contest (a publicity campaign involving photos, videos, and road trips) – but also lots of room for play. Since I had free gas, I drove to Boulder nearly every chance I got to hike my favorite trail, and visited friends in Denver once a week. I used my miles to schedule trips to Washington, D.C. and Tortola to visit friends, with enough left over for a trip to Chicago when my friend Loren and I won tickets to one of Oprah's last shows.

I couldn't have planned **all** of these happy occasions, but I certainly made room in my schedule (and my budget), and made the most of every opportunity for happiness. If tulips in the spring make you happy, and you have a patch of land and $20, make the time to buy some bulbs and put them in the ground! Your two-hour investment now will reap *days* of smiles as you watch them bloom a few months later.

Over months of jobhunting, I sent out resume after resume, only to face rejection after rejection. In between though, I had wonderful visits with friends, a dozen views from the top of Mt. Sanitas, opportunities to speak on behalf of my favorite charity, and I even checked off a few of my 40-by-40 milestones. For every disappointment, I had an opportunity for happiness waiting for me just around the corner, because I had made room for them in my life, and planned accordingly. This allowed me to "leapfrog" my way from one happy day to another, and keep my spirits up in between, because I always had something to look forward to. When I finally got an interview with an awesome company, I wasn't worn out from months of disappointments, and my positive attitude (despite the bleak economy) got me the job.

Tool #3: Bank It (Game Show Style)

The best advice I ever got was from a surfer. I had taken a trip to Bali to learn the fine art of hanging ten, and had been falling off my board for two days. I wasn't frustrated yet, but I *was* starting to think that maybe I just wasn't cut out for this level of athleticism. Suddenly, my instructor, Bude, who had been helping another client, splashed over to me, waving his arms. "I know why you keep falling!" he said excitedly. He looked at me very seriously and said, "You're trying to control the ocean." I stared at him, clueless. "You're gripping the board with your feet," he said, "You're trying to control the wave underneath you, but you can't control the ocean – it's too big. Control your*self*, control your *balance*, and you will be able to ride any wave." He smiled encouragingly and patted my shoulder – a surfing Yoda, right there in the middle of Indonesia. I got on my board and sure enough, when I focused more on keeping my balance and less on trying to control the board, I rode that wave like a pro. Well, maybe a semi-pro. I might have even turned a little.

Maintaining your contentment in life is a lot like surfing; it's probably why so many people attribute the sport to helping them find peace and happiness. Surfing teaches you to ride the wave as long as you can, to extend your happiness as long as possible. Surfers will wait *all day* for a good wave to ride, because it's those 30 or 40 seconds of bliss that makes all the wet thumb-twiddling worth it.

When you come across happiness – I mean, pure, unadulterated, blissful contentment – **ride it**. Ride it for all it's worth. Drink it in, savor every single second, and then *bank it*, like your winnings in a millionaire game show. When times are tough again, go back to that ride in your mind, and relive that wave, to remind you of why you're here, why you're sticking around. Accrue all the wonderful moments you can, so you can return to them in times of disappointment. There might be a lot of sitting around and waiting for happiness; there might be a lot of wipeouts and bone-crushing sandbars in the years ahead, but remember that those moments of happiness are out there too, waiting to be caught and ridden if you hang in there and stay balanced.

Tool #4: White-Knuckle It If You Have To

Sometimes, life just stinks. Everything is bad, bad, bad, and no amount of positive self-talk helps. When this happens, you just have to white knuckle it (i.e., hang on until the blood drains out of your palms).

I've had so many days in my life where all I could do is hang on – where I'm on autopilot, just putting one foot in front of the other until I get to a better place. You have to think of days like these like storms you just have to ride out. Think of any metaphor you like that works for you – nature has a million of 'em. In the end, it's just a waiting game, and you have to come up with tricks to help the time pass by. When I was in the hospital after a surgery, I remember just watching the minute hand turn on a clock, reminding myself that time passing is inevitable, and every second that little arm passed was a second closer to the moment when I felt better. Find your own ways to hang on, and put them in your medicine cabinet for those days when you can't remember how it felt to feel good, and it seems like forever until the next happy day.

Tool #5: If You Can't Hang On, Reach Out

I will be the first to admit that I made cancer look easy. Sure, I lost my hair, but I made YouTube videos and inspired women to get out there, baldness be damned. I drove myself to the doctor four times a week for chemo, blood draws, and neupogen shots, and never complained, because I didn't want people to feel sorry for me. I was afraid that if people felt sorry for me, I would start to feel sorry for *myself*. So I hung in there, I white-knuckled it, and I told everyone, "I got it." but you know what? I didn't got it. I didn't got it at all. And one day I found myself sitting in my living room, very close to giving up completely. Fortunately for me, I had friends who noticed, and threw me a life preserver before I had the chance to drown.

It's easy to say, "I got it," but don't let yourself get to a place where you've been hanging on so long that you don't have any strength left to ask for help when you need it. It takes a lot of courage to say, "I can't do this anymore," or "I can't do this by myself." Even if it's with the last of the strength you have in you, reach out, and if no one takes your hand, reach out farther, again and again, until someone does. Being brave enough to ask for help can save your life.

It is inevitable that you will make it through a tough time, only to face something just as tough later. I can't give you the formula for a life where nothing ever goes wrong, where no one ever disappoints you and everything is easy. It's going to take work to hang in there; it's going to take work to talk yourself out of a funk, and there may be days when you just can't do it, because you haven't had enough practice. Keep trying, though – I promise it gets easier (remember how you get to Carnegie Hall?). When you've mastered using all the tools in your arsenal, then you'll be ready to face your biggest challenge - rafting the whitewaters of life.

Chapter Twelve: Rafting The Whitewaters Of Life

"You don't drown by falling into water. You drown by staying there." – Robert Allen

I took a kayaking trip with First Descents this summer, a long-overdue adventure that's been on my list ever since my first camp with them. I initially balked at the thought of snapping myself into a kazoo-shaped piece of plastic just so I could try to make it through a Class III rapid without drowning (I mean, I had already beat cancer – did I really need to put myself in harm's way for *fun*?). Yet here I was, floating towards a maniacal-looking wave train on the Salmon River, miles from civilization. All I wanted was to be back in the inflatable "ducky" – a bigger, softer kayak that rolled over rapids like a monster truck at a state fair rally. I looked up at Corey, my safety boater and an amazing adventurer (let alone kayaker) in his own right, who grinned ear to ear and called out my FD nickname: "LEMON DROP!!" I took a deep breath and braced myself.

Joe Campbell says the hardest part of the Hero's Journey is the very last leg home, called "The Flight." This is where the forces of darkness, or Nazi army, or corporate lawyers bring in the big guns, because they see that the Hero is almost home. They see that he is within inches of triumphing, so they call out all the stops to scare him into giving up before he gets there. I call this chapter *Rafting the Whitewaters of Life* because it's about how to navigate **big** water. These aren't the day-to day strategies you're going to use for a Class I stream; these are the ones you'll need to turn to when you come around a bend and all you see is a football field of churning, swirling waves standing between you and your front porch.

Lesson One: Stay Loose

In the border between the main corridor of a river (where the water is multi-layered and moving fast) and the slower waters on either side of it (the "eddies") is a seam where water moving at two different speeds meets. Inevitably, this creates small little whirlpools all along that border, each one moving in a different direction. These are the "swirlies" – spinning little fuckers with choppy edges that can catch your kayak and throw you off balance in seconds. God, I hated those swirlies.

I flipped twice in the same eddy my first day in a hard shell. I would see a swirlie coming and immediately stiffen up, which is the worst thing you can do in a kayak. Stiffening up turns you into a sailboat without a keel – the slightest tilt to one side or another tips you right over. I would stiffen, the swirlie would catch the edge of my kayak, and down I'd go, every time.

My second day in a hardshell, Land (our fearless leader, who was channeling a young Jeff Bridges) realized right away what was going on in my head. "Don't look down!" he called out. "Don't look at the bow of your boat; look at me, look right here!" I took my eyes off the swirlies and looked just above them, to Land's mellow face. "Now paddle – don't let yourself move faster than the water underneath you, just paddle nice and gentle, and RELAX! Concentrate on keeping your body RELAXED!" Every time I saw a swirlie out of the corner of my eye, I would feel myself start to stiffen, and I'd hear Land's voice in my head – "RELAX!" – and take a breath and try to loosen up. It took a lot of effort – I felt like there wasn't one moment on the river that I wasn't concentrating – but the time it actually took me to relax got shorter and shorter, and pretty soon, the moment I started to stiffen, I would catch myself quickly and shake the feeling off before I could lose my balance.

When you're approaching what looks like a nightmare, what will prepare you best is taking a moment to RELAX. Focus all your attention on it. Don't let yourself stiffen up or you'll be frozen with fear, and unable to maneuver your way through anything. If something starts to terrify you, use all your energy to consciously think, "RELAX," and direct your focus to your first priority: staying loose.

Lesson Two: Master the Hip Snap

My most triumphant moment on the water wasn't making it past a Class IV rapid in an inflatable kayak. It was two days later, when, on my second day in a hard shell, I hip-snapped myself upright in the middle of a rapid, just in time to keep my kayak from flipping over. I did it twice, and in those moments, I realized I had the power to right myself, before I lost my equilibrium completely.

It's an amazing feeling, to right yourself, to keep yourself from going over. To save yourself. Of course it's okay to be rescued; of course it's okay to flip, wet exit, and swim to shore. But to be able to snap yourself out of it, in that moment where you're hanging between being upright and being upside down, that is a *beautiful* thing. It instantly made me less scared, not just of the water, but of kayaking. Before that moment, every minute in the river was a minute I could flip over – I was in a constant state of anxiety. After it, I felt just a little bit more confident that, if I started to lose my balance, I could regain it before I had to be rescued. I felt less at the mercy of the river, and less scared to be in it.

In kayaking and in life, when you can learn to catch yourself before going over, it gives you the confidence to trust yourself. When you trust yourself, you'll have faith in your ability to "right" yourself before everything turns upside down, and you can face the whitewaters of life without freaking out so much. Practice your hip snap, and get good at it, and when you see a field of churning waves before you, you'll have the confidence to paddle through it.

Lesson Three: Paddle Like You Mean It

I felt okay halfway through my first day in a hard shell. I had wet-exited twice and Hand-of-God-ed three times (this is when another kayaker literally comes up next to your upsidedown kayak and flips it upright with one arm), but it had been almost an hour since I'd flipped, and I had just made it through a gnarly rapid in one piece. I was taking a moment to pat myself on the back when I heard Corey call out to me from across the river, *"Lemon Drop! Get over here!"* I had drifted a little further out than I realized, and was headed for the wrong side of a bend.

I started to paddle, but I was fighting the current and my arms were exhausted from the rapids I'd just been through. "Lemon Drop, *paddle!*" Corey called out again, louder and more insistent. The current was picking up. I paddled harder, but I could feel the strength draining out of my muscles. I needed to get across the river, and fast. Corey started to paddle towards me, and then yelled at the top of his lungs, **"PADDLE LIKE YOU *MEAN* IT!"** I jerked up in my kayak and adrenaline flooded into my arms. I dug that paddle into the water like I was spreading peanut butter, and before I knew it, I was next to his kayak, breathing hard. He shook his head, grinning. "Really?" He said. "That was it? That was all I had to say?"

There will be a moments as you're rebuilding your life when you're almost to your breaking point. You'll feel like you don't have the strength to do what you need to do. In these moments, you have to dig deep and push yourself just beyond where you think you're capable, or you won't make it.

In these moments, remember, the way you do *anything* is the way you *everything*. If you've ever have had the strength to dig that deep, you still have it. All you need to call it out is the confidence that you can do it. When I find myself facing a challenge and feeling unsure of myself, I call up the memory of Corey yelling at me across the river, and I paddle like I *mean* it.

Kayaking is a lot like life – wave trains and rapids and waterfalls, and in between, the smooth lines of a calm river carrying you downstream. There are eddies and swirlies and a thousand opportunities to be turned upside down, but if you can get good at righting yourself, it can be the ride of your life. A river will teach you how to surrender, how to be strong, and most importantly, how to pay attention, so you know which one is required and when.

PART FOUR:
THE END OF THE JOURNEY

The Last Piece: Legacy

I heard the most wonderful story from a classmate, who commented on Xavier Rudd's cover of *No Woman, No Cry*. "You know," he said, "Bob Marley made sure that he shared the songwriting credit for this song with the soup kitchen in Trenchtown that he talks about in it, where they *'ate cornmeal porridge,'* so that every time someone covers it, every time the song is performed, the kitchen would get a cut of the profits." Now, every time I hear the song, it moves me to tears, thinking of how simple it was for Marley to leave something behind that would outlive him, that would keep giving back, literally forever.

We can't take anything with us, when our time is up here. We leave this world as empty-handed as we come into it, and when I came back from my biopsy, all I could think, looking around at a three-bedroom house full of furniture I'd paid thousands of dollars to ship across the ocean, was *"I am the only person this stuff matters to, and if I die, this is all going to end up at the Goodwill Thrift Store in Hanapepe."* I didn't even think of the friends and family who would be distraught, the future children I would never have, the husband I would never meet. Instead, I was struck by the ridiculousness of the loose ends I would leave behind, that my sister would have to tie up. All that time, effort, and money spent trying to create an environment I could grow old in, and cancer didn't give a crap about any of it. It seems so silly and frivolous now, looking back.

Remember Joe Campbell and the Hero's Journey? The last piece of the journey, when the Hero is home, when she's made it back from Mordor or cancer or the belly of the whale, is sharing her *boon* – what she's learned, what she fought the dragon to obtain – with the world. It's tough, because the Hero has to decide: keep the boon for herself, or give it to the world? In story after story, to become a Master of Two

Worlds, the Hero *must* turn the boon into a gift of service – a balm to heal the King, a message to bring peace, a treasure to save the town from demolition. To be a Hero, Campbell says, you cannot think only of yourself and your own gain. You must share your boon with the world.

Inevitably, we seek to understand the *why* of tragedy and disaster. **Why**, we ask. *Why did I go through this?* My answer is always, *to grow, to learn, to bring something back.* Learning to make lemonade out of lemons was like learning how to turn lead into gold for me, and without the lemons, I would never have that knowledge. Whatever you've been through, there is a lesson in it you can share with the world. Maybe it's advice for a friend going through the same thing. Maybe it's a class for schoolchildren, or a shelter for abandoned animals, or a work of art that speaks to a community. Your last task on this journey home is finding that lesson, turning it into an expression of what you've learned, and giving it back to the world in a way that makes it a better place.

In closing, remember, we all only have so much time here. When you start to craft a future worth living for, it's important to think about what you want to leave behind. Someday, even if that day is not today, you will be nothing but ashes and dust, so think about your legacy, and how you want to be remembered. Let *that* be the beginning of your *next* adventure.

Epilogue

I had an epiphany at the personal power camp my sister treated me to when I was in Development Hell. The instructor was lecturing on overcoming fear, and the importance of facing your fears, so they don't limit your potential. Later in the seminar, he also stressed the importance of giving back, saying, "You will never be rich if you cannot provide a service to someone." I thought of Campbell, and realized that if you could combine these two ideas – overcoming a fear and being of service – into a career, that it would be a rewarding, renewing occupation. Overcome a fear, and turn that into a service profession, and every day you will feel the thrill of mastery. Every day, you will watch other people as they triumph over the same fear that held you in its grip, and every day you will receive the gift of being a partner in *their mastery.*

When I took the class, the thing I was the most afraid of was letting people see me bald, puffy-faced, and "sick" – I looked in the mirror every day, and felt like an extra from *I Am Legend.* When I visited friends, I could not hide my hairlessness, my chest port scar, my *ill*-ness, and it made me incredibly self-conscious. Eventually, I stopped calling people to hang out, tired of worrying about my sickly appearance.

I got back from the seminar and realized this fear of what people would think about what I looked like **was** holding me back. It was literally keeping me from living my life, and adding to my sense of isolation and loneliness. I thought of what facing that fear and overcoming it would look like, and how I could turn that process into a gift of service. Who else felt like I felt? *Probably every woman out there in chemo,* I thought. *They're all holed up like me, watching TV because they're tired of drawing on eyebrows in an attempt to make a silk purse out of a sow's ear.* And then, suddenly, I had my answer. When I wanted to, I could pull it together – after all, I was pretty good at making lemonade, right? I *could* draw on eyebrows. I was pretty good at wrapping a scarf around my cue ball head. I took a cue from *Crocodile Dundee** and decided to make a

YouTube video, putting it all out there – my baldness, eyelash-less-ness, and cancer pallor. I put it out there for other women who were wondering how to not look like so much of a freak when they went grocery shopping during months of chemotherapy. When I finally published it on YouTube, it chipped away at my self-consciousness a little, and with every comment a user posted thanking me for sharing my vulnerability, I grew less and less afraid to let my friends see me "sick."

Five more videos later, my hair had started growing back, and I wasn't wearing baseball caps to cover my bald spots anymore. On my first day at work without a cap or scarf, I shared my nervousness about my appearance with our General Manager and he said, regarding my peach fuzz scalp, *"I love it! It's a celebration of life!"*

* There is a scene in *Crocodile Dundee* when Mick describes the Walkabout Creek version of "therapy": *"If you've got a problem, you tell Wally. He tells everyone in town, brings it out in the open… No more problem."*

Thank you for reading *Life After Lemonade*, by April Capil

If you enjoyed this book, please check out its prequel,
Recipe For Lemonade, available at Amazon.com,
BarnesandNoble.com and Smashwords.com.

Made in the USA
Charleston, SC
11 July 2013